Thomas S. Preston

The ark of the covenant

Thomas S. Preston

The ark of the covenant

ISBN/EAN: 9783337657260

Printed in Europe, USA, Canada, Australia, Japan

Cover: Foto ©ninafisch / pixelio.de

More available books at **www.hansebooks.com**

ARK OF THE COVENANT;

OR A

SERIES OF SHORT DISCOURSES UPON THE JOYS, SORROWS, GLORIES AND VIRTUES

OF THE

EVER BLESSED MOTHER OF GOD.

BY THE REV. THOMAS S. PRESTON.

"I will take hold of thee, and bring thee into my mother's house; there Thou shalt teach me."—Canticles, viii. 2.

New York:
P. O'SHEA, PUBLISHER, 104 BLEECKER,
AND 183 GREEN STREET.
1863.

Entered according to Act of Congress, in the year 1860,

By Rev. T. S. PRESTON,

In the Clerk's Office of the Southern District of New York.

INTRODUCTION.

The following chapters are intended either as short discourses, or as meditations upon the life of the Blessed Virgin.

They have been so arranged as to be suitable to the month of May, the first chapter being designed for the last day of April. But they have a general interest, and may be useful at any season of the year, since devotion to the holy mother of God is always the fruit of piety and a great means of sanctification. The different parts of the volume present continuously a brief history of the holiest and best of all God's creatures. The author puts forth this little book with a sincere desire to aid in the salvation of souls. He hopes to reach some hearts by the simple tale of Mary's joys and sorrows, and to beget in them a true love for virtue. If he can induce even one to imitate more closely the example which is here portrayed, he will have done enough. Amid constant occupations it has been to him a great consolation to say a word of gratitude in honor of her, whom from the depths of his heart he feels to be the cause of all his joy. May she but deign to accept this trifling and unworthy offering which he lays at her feet, and make it instrumental in advancing her interests and those of her Son.

T. S. P.

NEW YORK, *Feb.* 22, 1860.

CONTENTS.

CHAPTER I.
Preparation.............................. 11

CHAPTER II.
The Immaculate Conception—Day of Purity.. 17

CHAPTER III.
Th Birth of the Blessed Virgin—Day of Grace. 24

CHAPTER IV
The Presentation of the Blessed Virgin—Day of Consecration........................ 31

CHAPTER V.
The Annunciation of the Blessed Virgin—Day of Fidelity............................ 39

CHAPTER VI.
The Visitation of St. Elizabeth—Day of Mercy. 46

CHAPTER VII.
The Nativity of our Lord—Day of Life....... 54

CHAPTER VIII.
The Presentation of our Lord—Day of Praise. 61

CHAPTER IX.
The Prophecy of St. Simeon—Day of Fear.... 69

CHAPTER X.
The Flight into Egypt—Day of Self-sacrifice.. 77

CHAPTER XI.
The Loss of Jesus in the Temple—Day of Loneliness................................. 85

CHAPTER XII.
The Meeting of Jesus and Mary on the Way to the Cross—Day of Grief................ 93

CHAPTER XIII.
The Death of Jesus—Day of Remorse........100

CHAPTER XIV
The Piercing of the side of our Lord—Day of Gratitude 108

CHAPTER XV.
The Burial of Jesus—Day of Abasement......115

CHAPTER XVI.
The Resurrection of our Lord—Day of Illumination........................ 123

CHAPTER XVII.
The Ascension of our Lord—Day of Joy......130

CHAPTER XVIII.
The Coming of the Holy Ghost—Day of Peace.137

CONTENTS.

CHAPTER XIX.
The Death of the Blessed Virgin—Day of Victory.................... 145

CHAPTER XX.
The Assumption of the Blessed Virgin—Day of Union........ 152

CHAPTER XXI.
The Coronation of the Blessed Virgin—Day of Rest...................................160

CHAPTER XXII.
The Office of the Blessed Virgin............167

CHAPTER XXIII.
The Faith of the Blessed Virgin.............175

CHAPTER XXIV.
The Hope of the Blessed Virgin.............183

CHAPTER XXV.
The Charity of the Blessed Virgin...........191

CHAPTER XXVI.
The Humility of the Blessed Virgin..........199

CHAPTER XXVII.
The Purity of the Blessed Virgin............207

CHAPTER XXVIII.
The Poverty of the Blessed Virgin..........214

CHAPTER XXIX.
The Obedience of the Blessed Virgin........221

CHAPTER XXX.
The Patience of the Blessed Virgin..........229

CHAPTER XXXI.
The Prayer of the Blessed Virgin............236

CHAPTER XXXII.
The Union of the Blessed Virgin with God....244

CHAPTER I.

PREPARATION.

"In me is all grace of the way and of the truth ; in me is all hope of life and virtue."—Ecclesiasticus, xxiv. 25.

Such is the language of the Holy Spirit concerning the Blessed Mother of God. And among all her glories there is none greater than that of leading sinners in the way of life, and guiding the pilgrim to new heights of virtue. Indeed, as this is her especial glory, so it is her especial office. The human heart is weak, and naturally tends to things of earth, and has no power to seek the more rugged ways of self-discipline and virtue. The human intellect is dark, and with all its endowments it cannot see the true light which shines from God. It requires a divine grace to touch man's heart with a love that shall turn him from things sensible, and to enlighten his understanding with the truth for the enjoyment of which he was created. The Blessed Virgin is the channel through which God conveys to fallen man this grace of light and truth. Her prayers and intercessions bring down the grace of conversion, become the safeguard of the pilgrim in the perilous journey of life, and at last crown him with glory when the battle is over and Heaven is everlastingly won. She is the Second Eve, the Mother of the living race. Her eyes of grace are ever turned upon us poor exiles, until she has accomplished her work of bringing us home, and until she reveals unto us, in all his surpassing loveliness, the blessed fruit of her womb, Jesus. Many a soul receives the light of faith who never could have obtained that precious gift but through her prayers. Many a soul, ready to fall under the pressure of temptation, beneath the dark shadow of the adversary, finds instant relief and strength through the grace which she dispenses.

All good Catholics recognize this office

of the Blessed Virgin; and practical devotion to her is the peculiar characteristic of our religion. She has taken root among God's elect, and her power is in Jerusalem. She has fulfilled in the Church the language of Scripture: "I was established in Zion, and in the holy city, likewise, I rested, and my power was in Jerusalem. And I took root in an honorable people, and in the portion of my God, his inheritance, and my abode is in the full assembly of saints. I was exalted like a cedar in Libanus, and as a cypress tree on mount Sion. I was exalted like a palm-tree in Cades, and as a rose-plant in Jericho."* By the infidel and the heretic she is not honored, for they have no real belief in the mystery of her Son's Incarnation. But by Catholics she is honored and served, and in proportion as they love and imitate her, do they grow in God's grace and in a true devotion to our Blessed Lord.

To us, then, on this day, does the Mother of Grace make her appeal. A day of life

---

*Eccles. xxiv. 15—18.

and mercy is dawning upon our souls. Nature and grace are in harmony. The earth is robing herself in the verdure of spring, and fruits and flowers come forth to enjoy the smile of their Creator, as faint emblems of the quickening power of God's love in the human soul. The resurrection of nature is the image of what the Lord, who is the resurrection and the life, will do in our barren and wayward hearts. There is no voice speaking to us of the divine justice now, and the sinner may come without fear to the footstool of his offended but forgiving Father.

Whatever, then, be our condition before God, let us improve the graces of the season, and open our hearts to the light and mercy of our Lord. If we are not in a state of grace, now we have power to awake and purify our souls. Great mortal sins may weigh heavily upon us, pressing us down to earth, and making us the easy prey of new temptation. Our past is remorse, and our future is gloomy apprehension. There is no physician in this world who can heal our malady or bring peace to our desolated hearts. Yet the Mother of Mercy calls: "In me is all grace of the way, in me is all hope of life and virtue." Let us listen to her voice; and putting ourselves under her protection, let us arise and go unto our Lord, and say unto Him: "Father, I have sinned against Heaven, and in thy sight." The way shall be opened before us, and all obstacles shall, one by one, be removed. This month shall be to us the beginning of a new life, and shall end in our complete recovery and salvation. And even if through God's mercy we are free from deadly sin, we have all much need of the especial graces which are now offered to us. Are we not suffering in many ways from the effect of past sins? Are we not full of imperfections, which render us unfit to appear before God's presence? How very few of us live up to our consciences, and can bear the light even of our own self-examination. Yet God's all-searching eye is to be our judge. If we make up the record of the years that are past, we shall find a history of mercies despised and graces unimproved; and the little that has been done, seems to have been done rather against our will than by our free co-operation. Coldness and tepidity are only preludes to mortal sin, and we have, therefore, good reason to be alarmed by the indifference we feel in the pursuit of virtue. Many of us have received the Sacraments with great frequency, and still have made but little progress in self-discipline. We have always the same sins to confess, and the least close inspection shows us an amazing depth of pride and self-will. What shall we do, when God calls us, and we have to stand before Him, in whose sight the smallest imperfection cannot abide? This very month may be a crisis in the history of our souls. If it be well spent, its especial graces may avert some threatening temptation and awaken us to more careful lives. If it be neglected, the days of our spiritual life may be numbered. Let us, then, as we seek for salvation, prostrate ourselves before the footstool of the Mother of Mercy, and commit our cause to her hands. If our hearts be ready, she will do her work. She will bring our needs before the throne of her Divine Son, and we shall feel a power in spiritual things which we never have experienced. Let it be our constant prayer during this season of grace, that God would prepare our hearts to hear and obey all His inspirations.

CHAPTER II.

THE IMMACULATE CONCEPTION—DAY OF PURITY.

"Thou art all fair, my love, and there is no spot in thee."
CANT. iv. 7

We begin our meditations where God began His work of grace, with the first existence of our blessed Mother. From all eternity He had foreknown her, and from the hour of man's sad fall had predicted her. She was the promised seed of the woman, who should bruise the head of the serpent; the Second Eve, who should repair the losses of our first mother. God, whose infinite wisdom devised the way of our redemption, condescended to take our nature upon Him, and His first step in the gracious work was the preparation of a Mother. All our race were condemned, and under the original curse were subject to the tyranny of the devil. The tree was corrupt at its root, and the spring poisoned at its source. The children of the fallen Eve were exiles from Heaven. The work of redemption needed to be as complete as was the destruction wrought by sin. It began, therefore, by the removal of the original curse. A Virgin was conceived, free from corruption and pure as was our first Mother when she was placed in Paradise. Without this grace of redemption, she never could have been a Second Eve, and the Mother of a new and living race. The serpent who deceived the first Eve had no power over her, for she was the child of prophecy, who was to bruise his head. She was to overcome the devil in every point, and this she could not have done had she been at any time his child and slave by virtue of the original curse. Her own office, therefore, in the economy of redemption, required that she should be conceived without sin, and God was bound by the perfection of His own being to make a perfect work. But all this grace the Blessed Virgin was to have. because the Eternal Son of God had chosen her for His Mother. The Word was to be made flesh, to take our human nature and to unite it forever to His divine person. The incarnate Lord is no less the Son of Mary, than He is the Son of God. As He was therefore to take of the veritable substance of His Mother, so He was directly concerned in her honor or in her dishonor. Had she been the child of the fallen race, infected by the original curse, her ignominy would have passed to the dishonor of her Son. The spring of life would have gushed up from a polluted source, the stem of Jesse would have budded from a corrupting root. He, who is all purity, would have touched the defilement of the impure. The propriety of the incarnation demanded the grace of which faith teaches us, and Mary, with innocence redolent of the purity of Eden, is created for the honor of Jesus, to glorify Him by her holiness, and to be for Him an unspotted Mother.

Among all her joys, Mary had no greater joy than this of her pure conception. It was the foundation of her exalted holiness, by which she towered above the tall cedars of Libanus, and raised her Virginal head to the skies. She came into a world of sin and death. She saw around her sorrow and distress, the ruins and wrecks of a fallen world. She saw how God's great majesty was hourly outraged, and how His amazing love was spurned every moment by His own creatures. Yet with all this she had nothing to do. Her soul and body were fragrant with the incense of purity. She knew she had never offended her God, her first beginning and her last end. She was not one of the ruins of the first Paradise. Original sin weighs upon us with all its grievous burden. We no sooner come into the world than we begin to be offensive to God. Our souls suffer from the darkness of ignorance and from the stimulus of concupiscence. Our bodies are the prey of disease and death. And as soon as we arrive at the age of reason, when our opening faculties ought to expand in God's grace and for His glory, we begin by our wills to turn from holiness. Actual sin develops itself in all its bitterness, and with all its fruitful power of evil. How different from this sad history was Mary's life. No darkness ever weighed upon her understanding. No cloud ever came between the bright mirror of her soul and the light of God. She was the "bright reflection of the Eternal Light, a mirror without a stain." Her heart was never swayed by passion, nor was there ever a tumult to disturb the tranquil rest of her spirit. God's graces came, and they were all improved. God's blessed providence, like a shield, covered her, and from His will she never swerved. What a cause have we to bless and praise our great Creator for the purity of Mary! There was one heart in which the infinite majesty of God found a rest, one bosom in which the Incarnate Lord might find a home. With us the memory of the past is ever painful, for at every step we take in the divine life, we feel more keenly the ingratitude of former sins, and can never altogether banish the shadow which they throw upon our spiritual being. We are like sick men recovering from an exhausting fever, or like the maimed and wounded soldier returning from battle. Hence, our present loses its cheerfulness and joy. We are wearied by small endeavors, and go heavily, as if beneath a painful burden. And the future, which ought to be bright with hope, as it reveals the distant towers of the celestial city to which we journey, fills us rather with dread and an unquiet apprehension. There is no cross like the weight of sin, no joy to be compared to the blessedness of innocence. While then we meditate to-day on the Immaculate Conception of our Blessed Mother, let us seek to imitate her purity and to have part in her joy. We cannot be free from the infection of sin as she was, but we have been once washed from every defilement in the blood of her Son. Had we died in the cleanness of our baptism, Heaven would have been our immediate portion. Now by penance and prayer we must anew wash ourselves in the sacred blood which we have despised, until the heart of a child come back to us with the docility and purity of our new birth. This baptism of tears is our only hope, and God, who excites in us the desire for purification, will make that desire fruitful. The Immaculate Virgin, who is our example, will be our solace and protection. At her feet we must offer up every thought and word and work. Every intention must be placed in her hands, and through the virtue of her prayers we shall have courage to persevere and be generous with God. A healing, cleansing power shall be felt in our souls, going down to the very depths of our wants, and giving us no rest until we find union with Him whom we adore, until we are purified even as He is pure. For "We are now the sons of God, and it hath not yet appeared what we shall be. We know that when He shall appear we shall be like to Him, because we shall see Him as He is."*

CHAPTER III.

THE BIRTH OF THE BLESSED VIRGIN—DAY OF GRACE.

"When I was a little child, I was pleasing to the Most High."—OFFICE OF THE BLESSED VIRGIN.

As the whole life of our Blessed Lady was full of wonders, so her birth was especially marked by God's grace. Her holy parents, St. Joachim and St. Anne, were past age, and had almost relinquished their part in the hope of being the progenitors of the Messiah. Still they were firm believers in

*1 E. St. John iii 2.

the promise made to Abraham, Isaac and Jacob, and exact observers of all the ordinances of the Jewish law. Almighty God was preparing them for the exalted dignity which awaited them, and they were obedient to His graces. As Sarah waited long for the child of promise, and then became a mother by a miraculous providence, so St. Anne was to wait in hope and faith, and then by an especial dispensation to become the mother of the Queen of Heaven. He that waiteth for God shall never be disappointed, but shall in the end receive graces far beyond even his desire. So St. Anne had never dreamed of the honor which God gave her, but her patience and humility obtained a reward far beyond her hopes. And hence new glory was given to God, for although the Blessed Virgin was conceived in the ordinary manner, yet it was by especial and miraculous power.

We have already spoken of the Immaculate Conception, and now in the birth of our Blessed Lady we are to see some of its glorious consequences. The human soul is the direct subject of grace, while the body participates only in the effect of either the state of grace or the state of sin. So the soul of the Blessed Virgin came pure and spotless from the hand of her Creator, and by her especial privilege she was freed from all the effects of the original curse. Ignorance and darkness were not her portion, and hence from the first beginning of her existence she began to glorify God. "My soul doth magnify the Lord, and my spirit hath rejoiced in God, my Saviour." She was the child of grace, and was filled with grace from her mother's womb. She was able, moreover, to correspond with grace even before her birth, and to glorify God before her eyes were opened upon this sinful world. The fathers tell us that she had attained to great sanctity, and that at her birth she came into the world a marvel of the love and mercy of her Maker. Just, and true, and perfect are all the divine ways, and so the eternal Son, in preparing a Mother, could deny her no grace of which she was capable. St. Thomas says that the Blessed Virgin was full of grace in three ways. Her holy soul, from the beginning, belonged entirely to God. Her body was wholly sanctified in order that she might clothe the eternal Word with flesh, and she was the channel of grace for the benefit of the human race.

We see, therefore, how much she glorified the wisdom and goodness of God, and how her birth contributed to His praise. She came into the world not only pure and spotless in her soul, but united to her Creator and filled with His love. She did not see "through a glass in an obscure manner," for the mist that veils sensible things, and makes them attractive, was dissolved before the vision of her understanding. She saw God alone in all things, and she glorified every moment His adorable will. Her body was until then he most beautiful work of God's hands, the fit habitation of her sanctified soul. And when she opened her eyes upon nature and rested her infant head upon her aged mother's arms, God received an immense honor, such as He had never received before from any of His creatures. The brightest archangel in all his dazzling splendor was not so beautiful in His eyes as the infant grace of Mary, the child of promise, who had already wrestled victoriously with the strong adversary, who was fore-ordained the chosen Mother of his well-beloved Son. Over that cradle of the Immaculate, angels bowed themselves, while evil spirits fled away in terror. With her birth began a new day of grace for fallen man, and the long line of the living, regenerate race seemed in spirit to cluster around the birth-place of their Mother. The morning star arose, and the divine purposes were ripening, and the great work of man's redemption approached its completion. The beginning was the sure pledge and foretaste of the end. Mary was born full of grace for our sakes, in order that she might communicate it to her fellow-creatures. She was born holy; she was born to be the Mother of God; but she was also born to be our great intercessor with her Son, to shield us with her prayers, and to communicate to the church the benefits of the Incarnation and the Cross. While, then, in contemplating the glories of Mary's birth, our first thought is of God's honor, our second thought should be of the graces we have received in consequence of this very birth. On this day we should review our lives past, and count up the mercies we have to answer for in the great day of account. If we cannot answer for our thousand sins, how can we answer for our thousand graces? We have sinned against the light, and against the monitions of our own consciences. We have no excuse to plead for our wayward course, for God has all along been following us, and His Spirit has been continually calling us to repentance. We can see His hands in all the dispensations of His providence. Here He gave us joy, that by His goodness He might turn our hearts. Here He gave us affliction, that He might draw our affections from earthly vanities to an enduring good. No father ever followed an erring child with more patient affection than our Lord has followed us.

To use His own words, He has stood at the door of our hearts knocking, like a suppliant, for entrance, and we have more than once refused to let Him in. How unlike we are to our Blessed Mother, in whose heart every grace of God was fruitful! Yet even now it is the day of grace with us, and Mary calls to us by the beauty of her childhood, wholly consecrated to her Creator, to turn from the sins which have made so barren our spiritual life. Now God calls us, and gives the power to obey His call. Whether we be in the morning of life, or in the noonday of manhood, or in the evening of declining age, we have much to do before our probation closes. Time is short, and eternity is long. That which our hands find to do, let us do it with all our might, for the night cometh when no man can work. This sacred month will be to us a new responsibility, as it is a new grace from God, destined to effect the great end of our being, the salvation of our souls. Let us accept this merciful interposition of our Lord, and open our hearts, and stir up our wills to obey His call. The grace which filled the soul and body of the infant Virgin will overflow to us, and enable us to walk in her footsteps.

CHAPTER IV.

THE PRESENTATION OF THE BLESSED VIRGIN—DAY OF CONSECRATION.

"Arise, make haste, my love, my dove, my beautiful one and come."—CANTICLES ii. 10.

WE have seen how Mary was pure from every stain, and how her infant years were filled with God's grace; we are now to contemplate the fruits of her early sanctity in her immediate and entire consecration to the service of her maker. The Fathers tell us that the holy parents of the Blessed Virgin had made a covenant with God that the child, for whom they had so long prayed, should be dedicated to His service. When, therefore, so unexpectedly they received an answer to their prayers, they were not backward to fulfil their promise. Although the wonderful holiness and surpassing loveliness of their child had endeared her to their hearts, yet they could not resist the claim of God. They had nearly finished their earthly course, and full of faith in the covenant made with their fathers, were almost ready to find their rest in the bosom of Abraham, yet they were ready to give up the solace and glory of their declining days, content to make any sacrifice to which the Divine Providence called them. No parents had ever made such a sacrifice, and it was their consolation that they gave all they had to God, and that in so doing they made the most acceptable offering His Divine Majesty had ever received. They knew the value of their offering in their own eyes, but they did not then know its full value in the eyes of God. So he who walks by faith and in all things seeks only God, may often find that his feeble works have a value far beyond his imagination. Sacrifices cheerfully made are the highest proof that we are under the guidance of the Holy Ghost.

When the Blessed Virgin was only three years old, following her own wish and the Divine Inspiration, St. Joachim and St. Anne set out from Nazareth for Jerusalem. They took the holy child in their arms, and hastened to bear her to the altar of God. It was a long journey at their advanced age, yet He who was their guide was their support. They were consoled in their bereavement by the hope of the redemption of Israel, which was far nearer than their faith divined. They entered the temple and presented their offering at the foot of the holy altar. The priest, who, according to tradition, was Zachary, the father of St. John Baptist, received the child and offered her to God. The Blessed Virgin was filled with joy and with the Holy Ghost, and anticipating the act of her parents, she made a solemn consecration of herself to the service of her Creator. All her gifts, and all her faculties of soul and body, had ever been devoted to God, but now before men and angels she makes the open profession of her love. Here, according to the testimony of the fathers, she made the vow of virginity, choosing rather to renounce her hope of being the Mother of the Messiah, than to give up the imperishable glory of her immaculate purity. What was the world to her? Nothing human had power to draw her heart from Heaven and the world of grace in which she lived. She heard the voice of her celestial spouse: "Arise, make haste, my love, my dove, my beautiful one, and come." "One is my dove, my perfect one is but one; she is the only one of her mother, the chosen of her that bore her. The daughters saw her and declared her most blessed, the queens and concubines, and they praised her. Who is she that cometh forth as the morning rising, fair as the moon, bright as the sun, terrible as an army set in array."*

It is an unspeakable consolation to think of the great glory which God received on this auspicious day. No created thing had ever

---

* Canticles vi. 8—9.

paid Him such honor. Angels in all their purity had prostrated themselves, and cherubim and seraphim had veiled their faces before His unapproachable Majesty, yet never had He received a worship as acceptable as this worship of Mary. She was pure as the crystal waters of Paradise, and as she knelt in all humility, all Heaven seemed to rest upon her, and the three persons of the Eternal Trinity were bowed in condescension upon that little child. Wonderful spectacle, full of joy both for Heaven and for earth. God accepted her vow, and received her for His own, and she became the Queen of that Virgin train that "follow the Lamb withersoever He goeth."

There are two important lessons for us to learn on this day. God requires us to consecrate ourselves to His service, and to do it with the dispositions which made Mary's offering so acceptable. In whatever state we are called to work out our salvation, consecration is the essence of the religious life. God demands our hearts, and will accept nothing less from us. We are consecrated by baptism and emancipated from the tyranny of the world, the flesh, and the devil. Thrice happy are they who can retire from all things earthly, to espouse themselves, like Mary, to Him whom the angels serve. Yet, in every walk, the christian life is essentially the same. We cannot hope to save our souls except our consecration be entire. And this embraces the devotion of our affections and the oblation of every faculty of soul and body. We cannot serve God and the world, or hope to win Heaven when our affections are fastened on earthly things. And how few are there in any walk of life who are equal to this consecration! The world is ever interfering between our souls and God, and we are easy victims to its snares. We try to persuade ourselves that we are living for Heaven, while in reality every day augments our account of pride and self-will, and human respect. No one but God can sound the depths of deceit and self-seeking, which are found in the human heart. Let us pray our Lord to prove and try us, and to see if "there be any way of iniquity in us, and to lead us in the way eternal."

But we are bound not only to consecrate ourselves to God with the perfect devotion of every faculty; we are also called to imitate the dispositions of our Blessed Mother. She gave every thing to God, and she gave all immediately, reserving no will of her own. Her heavenly master called, and she obeyed without consulting with flesh and blood. So when we make our offering we should place no limitations to our gift. We should reserve nothing, no creature, no corner of our hearts. God may take us at our word, and then we should leave all in His hands, convinced that His will can only work out our highest good. This is the royal road of sanctification. And when He speaks to our souls we should listen to His voice. It is the music of Heaven. And when we hear we should instantly obey. O, what heights of virtue are within our reach! What numberless graces all depending upon our consent! The more carefully we listen, the more often God will speak, until at last He becomes our ever-present guide, making all our repose, and peace, and happiness. Let us come, then, to-day to Mary's altar with our oblation. Let us place ourselves in her hands. Let us ask for the same spirit of consecration which she had, and beg her to present us before her Son. To Him let our future lives be dedicated. For Him let us breathe every breath, speak every word, and do every action. He will accept repentance for the past, if there be only a steady will for the present, and a firm resolve for the future. Let us say with the royal psalmist, "For what have I in Heaven, and besides Thee what do I desire upon earth? For Thee my flesh and my heart have fainted away. Thou art the God of my heart, and the God that is my portion for ever."*

*Psalm, lxxii. 26.

CHAPTER V.

THE ANNUNCIATION OF THE BLESSED VIRGIN—DAY OF FIDELITY.

"The voice of my Beloved, behold He cometh, leaping upon the mountains, skipping over the hills."—CANT. 2—8.

The whole early life of the Blessed Virgin had been spent in the uninterupted service of God. From the hour of her consecration in the temple she had no thought but of Him, and no wish but to do His will in all things. Her soul was enlightened to see God, and filled with the continual contemplation of His perfections. No human mind can imagine the perfection to which she had attained; but we know that no creature had ever received such graces, and that every grace was improved to her sanctification. In the temple, before the altar, assisting at the daily sacrifice, she prayed constantly for the redemption of Israel. She prayed for the coming of the Messiah. As she has since revealed to St. Elizabeth, she prayed that she might live to see the mother of the Christ, and that she might serve her with her own hands, and praise her with her lips, and minister to her necessities. She knew by the prophets that the day of redemption was drawing nigh, and she was so taken into the counsels of God that she could see His purposes ripening every day. As the hour of the Incarnation approached, the Divine Providence directed that she should be espoused to St. Joseph. That holy and spotless Saint had been chosen for her protector, and she consented to the espousals, fully understanding that nothing should ever infringe upon the sovereign right of her celestial spouse. God's will was her only rule, and St. Joseph was to her only an image of the Eternal Father, before whom every wish was bowed in obedience. It is almost a foretaste of Heaven to contemplate this life of Mary, and to think how she was glorifying God. And the Infinite Majesty was drawn by her very loveliness, and the Divine eyes looked away even from the rapt adoration of Seraphim and Cherubim, of all the angelic host, to rest upon His meek handmaiden, whose worship was more pleasing to Him than that of all the armies of His courts. So grew this "fair plane-tree by the waters, yielding a sweet smell like cinnamon, and stretching out her branches of honor and grace." She was only fourteen years old, and in the perfect beauty of womanhood, when the fullness of time came, and that, which her humility has never dared to anticipate, was accomplished. God was coming not to take up His abode in her heart, for there long had He dwelt, but to become in very truth her child. All humble, all unconscious of her dignity, she knelt in the temple, praying for more and more perfect union with her Beloved, when at once all the light of sense seemed to depart, and the bright light of Heaven to come in upon her soul. The Archangel Gabriel knelt before her, and the pinions of unseen angels covered her, and the celestial messenger spoke his "Ave Maria." "Hail Mary, full of grace, the Lord is with thee, blessed art thou among women."* Then he revealed to her the mystery of the incarnation, and how she had found favor with God, and had been chosen of all the daughters of earth to become the mother of the Most High. There was one moment of fear and suspense, until she was assured that neither her sacred vow of virginity should be violated nor her immaculate purity sullied. Then, meekly and humbly, she consented to this new and incomprehensible grace, with all its trials and with all its glories. "Behold the handmaid of the Lord, be it done to me according to thy word." Then the Holy Ghost came upon her, and the power of the Most High overshadowed her. Who can describe the joy of this blissful moment, far surpassing all the consolations of the saints? A more than angelic ecstacy overwhelmed all the powers of soul and

---

* St. Luke, i. 28.

body, and her God, her Beloved, came leaping upon the celestial mountains, skipping over the hills of earth, and in an instant He was not only her Creator—He was her child. Before her enraptured vision was the sight of the eternal Trinity, and in her soul that grace of perfect union which no tongue can describe. Well might she say, "I languish with love. His left hand is under my head, and His right hand shall embrace me."* Alas, our faith is feeble, and our intellect staggers, and we can never measure the length and breadth and depth and height of this great mystery. We cannot measure the condescension of the Divine Majesty—we cannot measure the infinite elevation of Mary. If it is a joy to possess God as He reveals Himself to the elect ; if it is bliss to know Him as the angelic spirits whom He ravishes with a torrent of untold delight, what must have been Mary's joy at this awful moment? She found, in an ineffable way, her Beloved whom she sought. She could never be

* Canticles, ii. 5, 6.

separated from Him. She was nearer to Him than any other creature ever could be, and the mountain tops of heroic sanctity were nothing to her elevation. She was folded in the complacency of the eternal Trinity, the daughter of the Father, the mother of the Son, the spouse of the Holy Ghost. We behold, therefore, on this day, the accomplishment of the primeval prophecy and the actual redemption of our race. We see the faithfulness of God, who in His own good time fulfils all His promises. The covenant with Abraham and Isaac and Jacob was kept notwithstanding the ingratitude and rebellion of nearly the whole chosen nation. The light which the prophets saw at a distance was the divine light. "A virgin had conceived," and the name of her child was Emmanuel, "God with us." The faith of the patriarchs was realized, and the first Adam, who was only a living soul, rejoiced in the coming of the second Adam, a quickening spirit, the Lord from Heaven. And Mary's great dignity was also a reward to her fidelity.

She had never disobeyed even in thought the will of God. She had made good use of every grace, and it was her recompense not only to be united to the Author of Life, but to conceive in her chaste womb Him whom the Heaven of Heavens cannot contain. So the Master whom we serve is always better than His promise, and if we were only faithful to Him, we should obtain joys of which this world has no knowledge.

How often has God sought us, and in how many thousand ways has He shown His especial favor toward us!

His advances have been met by coldness, indifference, or ingratitude. He has sought to unite Himself to us, and we have sought the friendship of the world, the satisfaction of our own pride, and the gratification of passion. Let us learn by Mary's fidelity, and her great reward, to correspond more faithfully to the divine mercy toward our souls. The voice of our beloved Redeemer is really calling us. Let us seek to return to Him some of that love which He has so squandered upon our ungrateful hearts.

CHAPTER VI.

THE VISITATION OF ST. ELIZABETH—DAY OF MERCY.

"Whence is this to me, that the mother of my Lord should come to me."—St. Luke, i. 43.

It is not for us to know the unspeakable delight which ravished the soul of the Blessed Virgin while she was bearing her God in her chaste womb. She enjoyed a nearness to God of which no creature can have a just conception, and the Holy Ghost has not been pleased to reveal much of the blessedness of her interior life. We are to contemplate to-day one of her acts of charity, by which she was made the minister of grace to others, and by which God testified to the coming of His Son. Her cousin, St. Elizabeth, had conceived a child in her old age, and the circumstance was well known to the Blessed Virgin. The archangel Gabriel, who came to her on the glad mission, which had been the cause of all her joy, had been a messenger to Zachary, foretelling the birth of the forerunner of her son. And Zachary had been unable to tell of the heavenly vision; for the angel, to punish him for his doubt, and also to give a sign to his faith, had closed his lips until the prophecy should be accomplished. St. Elizabeth had conceived, and was now in the sixth month of her pregnancy, when our Lord incited His mother to visit her for the manifestation of His power and glory. And "Mary rose up and went with haste into the mountainous country, to Hebron, a city of Juda." It was the impulse of the Holy Ghost which she obeyed with alacrity. She entered into the house of Zachary and saluted Elizabeth. This salutation was like a divine voice to her ears. The "infant leaped in her womb," and she "was filled with the Holy Ghost." The forerunner received strength to pay homage to the Messiah, and Elizabeth felt the presence, not of her cousin, but of the mother of her God. She cried out with a loud voice. The Eternal Spirit spoke through her lips. "Blessed art thou among women, and blessed is the fruit of thy womb. And whence is this to me that the mother of my Lord should come to me? For, behold, as soon as the voice of thy salutation sounded in my ears, the infant in my womb leaped for joy. And blessed art thou that hast believed, because those things shall be accomplished that were spoken to thee by the Lord."* The uninterrupted ecstacy of the holy Mother then took a higher strain, and she spake her more than angelic *Magnificat:* "My soul doth magnify the Lord, and my spirit hath rejoiced in God my Saviour. Because He hath regarded the humility of His handmaid; for behold from henceforth all generations shall call me blessed. For He that is mighty hath done great things to me, and holy is His name. And His mercy is from generation to generation, to them that fear Him. He

* St. Luke, i. 42–5.

hath showed might in His arm ; He hath scattered the proud in the conceit of their heart. He hath put down the mighty from their seat, and hath exalted the humble. He hath filled the hungry with good things, and the rich He hath sent empty away. He hath received Israel His servant, being mindful of His mercy, as He spake to our fathers, to Abraham and his seed for ever."* Wonderful words, fit for the Mother of God to magnify her Lord and Saviour. And Mary abode with St. Elizabeth about three months, discharging the office of charity, and instructing her in the ways of the divine providence, and then returned to her own house in Nazareth. Such is the simple scripture narrative of the visitation of the Blessed Virgin. The Holy Ghost has thought it so important that it could not be passed over in silence, among the many things concerning our Lord which never have been written. Almighty God by it testified to the dignity of His mother and the truth of His incarnation. It was by no

* St. Luke, i. 46—55.

human power that Elizabeth saw in her meek and humble cousin the Mother of God. Flesh and blood never have revealed to any soul this great mystery. The Holy Ghost opened her eyes, and put upon her lips the words which were to be echoed in the church forever after, forming the joy and solace of all the faithful: "Blessed art thou among women, and blessed is the fruit of thy womb, Jesus." St. John the Baptist, too, was miraculously conceived, that he might go before the Redeemer to prepare His way. An infant in his mother's womb, he had strength to feel the presence of the Lamb of God, and to adore Him, and to testify, even before his birth, to Him for whom he was to live and die. And Mary, not only for herself, but for us and for all her children, exulted in the work of redemption, and taught us the strain of lowly praise which ever finds acceptance in the ears of the Most High.

By this wonderful event also, the Blessed Virgin discharged her office of minister of grace to others. It was her voice that awoke the faith of Elizabeth and caused her to be filled with the Holy Ghost. Her steps brought the Son of God to the adoration of His forerunner, and caused him to be sanctified in his mother's womb. For according to the common tradition of the church, St. John was then purified from original sin, and made pleasing to God. Hence we celebrate his holy nativity because he was born in grace. Mary was the instrument through which God was pleased to confer these favors. She was made the channel of new and wonderful grace to Elizabeth and her child. Her visitation was the day of unspeakable mercy to all that household. So is it ever. Where Mary comes, divine grace attends her steps; and wherever she goes, her Son goes with her. She brings to us the blessed fruit of her womb, the Author of Life. She confirms our faith, strengthens our hope, and teaches us how to love. She is the morning star of our early life, shedding its ray of purity over the dangers of our opening years, the bright sun of our noonday, driving away the shadows from the path of anxious manhood, and the evening light, purpling the decline of our day and illuminating the clouds of our sunset. She is our shelter in storm and tempest, a strong army in battle array in the hour of conflict. Her visitations of our soul are days of mercy, and if we improve them, they will end in an eternal and unbroken day. No doubt we can recall many such visitations. She has spoken to us when good desires came pouring in upon our hearts, when the shadow of the adversary darkened our path and blinded our vision, when the sight of our numberless infidelities almost destroyed our courage. After a fall she has come to us with her cheering words, and she has ever been at the foundation of any work we have raised for God. This day and this month she visits our souls. She finds little in them to attract her, but the hope of making them fit tabernacles for her Son to dwell in, the hope of redeeming them from the misery of sin to His endless praise. The voice of her salutation sounds in our ears. It will fill us with the Holy Ghost. It will detach us from the world and our besetting sins. It will nerve us against the temptation which now threatens us, and help us to a complete conquest of ourselves. Let us listen to this voice and follow its counsels, and make haste to render ourselves worthy of our spotless guest, that she may not only visit us but abide with us. "He that findeth her, findeth life, and shall obtain salvation from the Lord."* For she enricheth them that love her and filleth their treasures.

* Proverbs, viii. 35.

CHAPTER VII.

THE NATIVITY OF OUR LORD—DAY OF LIFE.

"My Beloved to me, and I to Him, who feedeth among the lilies."—CANTICLES, ii. 16.

THE joy of our Blessed Lady had been great during the nine months in which she bore her God in her sacred womb. We are now to contemplate another joy. She is to bring forth her Beloved, that she may know him by sense and feast her eyes upon His celestial beauty. As the day of her delivery approached, a heavenly messenger was sent to St. Joseph to acquaint him with the mystery of the incarnation, and to teach him his duty towards the lowly virgin and her child. Prophecy declared that the Messiah should be born in Bethlehem, the house of the true Bread. "And thou, Bethlehem Ephrata, art a little one among the thousands of Juda: out of thee shall He come forth unto me that is to be the ruler in Israel: and His going forth is from the beginning, from the days of eternity."* The Blessed Virgin was sojourning at Nazareth, when the Roman Emperor Cæsar Augustus was made the instrument in fulfilling the designs of divine providence. An imperial decree was issued that the whole empire should be enrolled. "And all went to be enrolled, every one to his own city." St. Joseph and the Blessed Virgin were both of the family of David, and they were obliged to go to Bethlehem, the city of David, there to register their names. So the very words of prophecy were fulfilled, and the birth of the Messiah and His descent were registered in the archives of the nation. Augustus only meant to enumerate his subjects, but among them was numbered his God. The holy family then began their wonderful journey. We can well imagine how full were the hearts of Joseph and Mary with heavenly conso-

* Micheas, v. 2.

lation. All the hopes of the patriarchs and prophets were now to be realised. The true Bread of Life and Hope of Israel was with them, and they were to see what seers and kings had so long desired. They came to the city already crowded with the descendants of David, and there was no room for them in the inn. They sought refuge in a cave where the beasts of the field were sheltered, and there, at the high hour of night, the Holy Mother, by a painless birth, and in an ecstacy of joy such as she had not before known, brought forth her child. The Evangelist has told us something of the wonders of that night. The whole creation seemed instinct with new life and ready to acknowledge its Lord. Shepherds were watching upon the hills, and they saw the angels who kept vigil, and heard their song: "Glory to God in the highest, and on earth peace to men of good will."* "Fear not, for behold we bring you good tidings of great joy which shall be to all people. For this day is born to you a Saviour, who is

St. Luke, ii. 14.

Christ the Lord, in the city of David." They saw the joy of the heavenly host, which in countless numbers filled the skies, and they were filled with their faith, and caught something of their joy. "They came with haste to Bethlehem; and they found Mary and Joseph, and the infant lying in a manger."* They paid Him their adorations, and "returned glorifying and praising God for all the things they had heard and seen." This is but a brief description of the rapture of the angels and the worship of the shepherds. But who can describe the transports which overwhelmed the soul of our Blessed Lady? She experienced a mother's joy heightened to an intensity no one else can know, for the little child was not only her own flesh and blood, He was also her God. Who shall tell of that first embrace in which her mother's heart overflowed, in which with lowly praise she adored her Creator and loved Him with a love no saint or angel had ever given Him? She took His tiny hands in hers, the hands

* St. Luke. II. 16.

which held at that moment the weight of the world. She pressed Him to her bosom and listened for the beating of that divine heart filled with all the tenderness of God. She looked into His face, and saw the likeness of her own features lighted with all the radiance of deity. She gazed lovingly and adoringly into those eyes which in all their infant innocence were looking back her love, and she knew they were reading the secret of her heart and the wealth of affection treasured up in her bosom. Well might she say, "My Beloved to me and I to Him," for now who should separate her from her child? He was hers, and she was to nourish His infant life, to support His tender years, to be ever with Him. She looked around upon the stable which He had chosen for a birth-place, and though she felt the indignity He received from an ungrateful world, yet to her that poor cave was brighter than the gilded palaces of kings. It was the gate of Heaven; it was even Heaven itself, for there was the great king and His mother, St. Joseph, the purest of the patriarchs, and the angels who had ever veiled their faces before His throne. And Mary rejoiced not only in her own great privilege, but also in the effect of this wonderful nativity. She saw by faith the redemption of the world, and felt the power of that new life which was to be the regeneration of man. The light had come into the world and the way of Heaven was opened to all believers. God became the Son of man, that we might become the sons of God. "To as many as received Him, to them He gave power to become the sons of God."* Because of his birth, we have been new-born in baptism, and because He lives, we have a spiritual life whose end is the vision of God. As often, therefore, as we think of the birth of Christ, our thoughts should go back to our own regeneration. The likeness of His spotless infancy was impressed upon us, and if we have lost that likeness, it is because our own hands have defaced the work of God. We shall never find peace until that likeness be restored to

* St. John, 1. 12.

us with its meekness, guilelessness, and docility. Devotion to our Lord's nativity will be one great mean of affecting this restoration. Let us ask the holy Mother to obtain for us this grace. And we may be sure there is no sinner beyond the reach of her prayers. The way of life is opened, and no matter how far we have wandered, we can find a safe return Let us pray the Blessed Virgin, by the joy she experienced when first she gazed upon her new-born child, to gain for us a complete recovery from sin and a new birth unto holiness.

CHAPTER VIII.

THE PRESENTATION OF OUR LORD IN THE TEMPLE—DAY OF PRAISE.

"While the King was at his repose, my spikenard sent forth the odor thereof."—CANTICLES, 1. 2.

EVERY day of our Lord's life was a day of grace to His mother. She was ever learning from Him new lessons, as she saw more and more of the counsels of God. Not only had the shepherds of Judea been to adore Him, but sages and kings from the far East had been led to His cradle by the "star that arose in Jacob." All these things gave Mary more and more of the spirit of her Son, and she was able to co-operate with Him in the great work for which He came on earth. We are to consider to-day how her humility and obedience united in a new act of praise to God.

Forty days after the birth of her child she went to the temple in Jerusalem, there to pay the customary offering for her purification, and to present her Son before the altar. She had no need of this ceremony, for she was not subject to the provisions of the law. Her child was miraculously born and her virginity remained untouched. She was "a garden enclosed, and a fountain sealed." Nevertheless, she was not disposed to take any advantage of her privilege, for the impulse of the Holy Spirit led her to the temple, to edify the whole world by her obedience, and to fulfil the prophecy of the old law. She appeared then with St. Joseph and the child Jesus before the altar, and asked for no distinction among the crowd of worshippers. She brought the offering of the poor, a pair of turtle-doves; and, sinless among sinners, pure among the impure, she knelt with her child before His own altar. It is hard for us, who are ever over-estimating our gifts and privileges, to understand such humility. No saint ever practiced such an heroic act of self-abnegation. The Mother of God comes with an offering for her purification, and bears reverently her God into His own temple! But God left not her great humility unrewarded. She was not to kneel there surrounded by hosts of adoring angels and yet unknown to the world. There were some chosen hearts waiting for the consolation of Israel, who were to echo the salutation of her cousin Elizabeth, and to see the salvation of the Lord, the Word made flesh. St. Simeon had long wept over the desolations of Jerusalem, and long had prayed for some token of the promise made to Abraham, Isaac, and Jacob. To him the Holy Ghost had revealed that before death should close his eyes he should see face to face the Christ of the Lord. The same Holy Spirit led him now into the temple, to the feet of the Blessed Virgin. His aged eyes were quick to see the presence of his God. His heart overflowed with joy as he saw the long-expected child, and his faith obtained a reward he had never hoped for. He was allowed not only to see his God, but to embrace Him in his arms. His days were almost spent; the shadows of evening were thick upon him, and he was soon going to rest in the bosom of the patriarchs. But now the Sun of justice shone upon his decline and made his rest glorious. Who can tell the ecstacy of his bursting heart, when, filled with the Holy Ghost, and with the Lord of Life pressed to his bosom, he spake his *Nunc Dimittis*: "Now, dost Thou dismiss Thy servant, O Lord, according to Thy word, in peace. Because mine eyes have seen Thy salvation, which Thou hast prepared before the face of all people, a light to the revelation of the Gentiles, and the glory of Thy people, Israel."* Could he ever forget, through all eternity, the illumination which then filled his soul, or the light which, dispelling the shadows of the valley of death, cast its rays far into the future of his glory? He could now go to the patriarchs and prophets to tell them that their deliverer was come, and to await His triumphant

---

* St. Luke, ii. 27—32.

ascension to open Heaven to all believers. It was reward enough for Mary to see this public recognition of her Son, and to hear the thanksgiving of St. Simeon mingled with the praises of Anna, the prophetess, as she "spake of Him to all who looked for the redemption of Israel." Yet she understood well the more sublime meaning of the great oblation she made. The great prophecy of Aggeus found its completion in her hands. The second temple, rebuilt after the captivity, was unworthy of comparison with the first great temple of Solomon. Yet it was to be made far more glorious by the presence of the Lord of Hosts, who in substance of our flesh was to tread its pavement and kneel before its altar. "Who is left among you," said the prophet, "that saw this house in its first glory? And how do you see it now? Is it not in comparison to that as nothing in your eyes? Yet, now, take courage, for thus saith the Lord of Hosts, yet one little while, and I will move the heaven and the earth and the dry land. And I will move all nations, and the desired of all nations shall come, and I will fill this house with glory. Great shall be the glory of this last house more than of the first, saith the Lord of Hosts, and in this place will I give peace."* This great event, so long predicted, and expected with so much fervor by all the faithful, now found its fulfilment. The second temple was filled with glory. Angels and archangels crowded its hallowed precincts to welcome the entrance of the king of glory. Almighty God was there, not now in shadow, or by sign or symbol, but in very deed and truth, the Second Person of the Eternal Trinity, the Word made flesh. He came there in His Mother's arms, in humble poverty, to claim His own, and to receive the worship which for ages had gone up to His throne. To Him was offered there the adoration of all faithful hearts, crowned with the acceptable homage of His holy mother's prayer. Yet He came not only to take possession of His own temple. He came there to make His grand oblation as the victim of

* Aggeus, ii. 4—10.

salvation, and the Blessed Virgin was the priest at this great ceremony. He chose to be offered in His infant years, and in His mother's arms. Here, then, was an oblation which recalled all God's promises. All the sacrifices of the just, from that of righteous Abel down to the victim whose blood had that morning moistened the mercy-seat, had derived their value from this great oblation. The mysteries of the incarnation and of the cross were brought together. The reality was to take the place of shadows. Around the child Jesus hung the darkness of Mount Calvary, proclaiming Him the saving Host, before whom every knee must bow in heaven and upon earth. When, therefore, the pure hands of Mary uplifted her child in the temple, she offered the great mediator between God and man. She made a sacrifice of expiation, thanksgiving, and praise, such as never before had ascended to the heavenly throne. It was by His merit that she had been kept pure from every defilement of sin. What other offering had she but Him who had made all her joy, and who alone could express her gratitude? For all God's mercies to her soul, she could only give back the child He had given her, and in so doing she made a sacrifice of infinite value. The presentation of our Lord in the temple appeals forcibly to our hearts. Mary's oblation, so precious in the sight of Heaven, was made not only for herself but for all her children. He is our victim of salvation. He only can interpose between our sins and the divine justice. He only can worthily thank and praise the Most High for the mercies of redemption. Let us enter into the heart of our holy mother, and with her pure desire for God's glory, shelter ourselves under the great oblation which she made. Let us praise our heavenly Father for all the graces He has lavished on our souls, but above all, that He has provided for us an offering worthy of His acceptance, His incarnate Son, our Lord Jesus Christ.

CHAPTER IX.

THE PROPHECY OF ST. SIMEON—DAY OF FEAR.

"I arose up to open to my Beloved; my hands dropped with myrrh, and my fingers were full of the choicest myrrh."—CANTICLES, v. 5.

HERETOFORE we have seen the Blessed Virgin in some of the joys which overflowed her soul. We are now to contemplate some of the sorrows which pierced her heart, and like great mountains cast their shadow over her sinless life. With the one exception of our Lord, no one ever suffered so much, and if her joys are far above our comprehension, her sorrows still more tower to the skies and are full of the mystery of divine providence. Of herself she merited no pain, for her sinless body and illuminated soul were ever pleasing to God. All her woes were on account of her maternal relations to the Eternal Word, and because she was so taken into the counsels of God that she participated in the great agonies of her Son. This consideration gives all her griefs an additional value in the sight of heaven, and constitutes a moving claim to our gratitude and love. She came so near to her Redeemer that He was her child and all His sufferings were hers. He could not suffer without her, nor could she be in grief without adding a new pang to His sacred heart. Her first great sorrow took place at a moment of great joy and exultation. St. Simeon had adored the child Jesus as the hope of Israel, and she had offered Him to His eternal Father in the spirit of self-sacrifice. The Holy Ghost chose this fitting opportunity to publicly reveal the consequences of this great oblation. "The Light had shone in darkness and the darkness did not comprehend it." The aged prophet saw in the distance the cross of Calvary, and gazed a moment into Mary's great depth of woe. He gave back his God into the arms of His mother, His fit resting-place, and full of grief at man's rejection of his deliverer, he prophesied, "Behold this child is set for the ruin, and for the resurrection of many in Israel, and for a sign, which shall be contradicted. And thine own soul a sword shall pierce, that out of many hearts thoughts may be revealed."* Here, then, before the eyes of the Holy Mother, came a clear view of the sufferings her child was to undergo. The prophecy seemed to gather up all her woes in one, and as anticipation often gives greater pain than the reality, a flood of grief overwhelmed her soul. She trembled as she gazed into the yawning gulf, but lost not for an instant her tranquil trust in God. There can be no doubt that she had long foreseen the clouds that hung over her wonderful life, and knew from the prophets that Emmanuel was to be "despised and rejected of men, a man of sorrows and acquainted with infirmity." The Holy Ghost now placed the whole picture before her. She saw, step by step, His way of the cross, the

* St. Luke, ii. 3, 4, 5.

ruin and rejection of her own guilty nation, and her own sad bereavement. She heard the voice of her Beloved; she arose up quickly to open to Him, and the mantle of His sorrows covered her. "Her hands dropped with myrrh and her fingers were full of the choicest myrrh." She touched His inconceivable woe, and flesh and heart would have failed, but the everlasting arms were under her, and God, who was so near, upheld her. Her infant, so dear to her, was to be the object of man's most cruel rage and persecution. As He began His life in a stable, so was He to end it upon a cross. She took her treasure home and gathered Him safe to her bosom, but there around His godlike brow were ever the prints of His thorny crown. On His hands and feet she ever saw the print of the nails, and when His heart was beating against her own, she was startled by the thought of the centurion's spear. Gladly would she have saved Him from all these ignominies by ten thousand sacrifices of her life, if that were possible. But she had made her great oblation, and she could not recede from it. **Every day, which made Him more lovely in her sight, brought Him nearer to His work of pain, and she could never dwell upon present joy without the fearful foreboding of coming grief.** Thus early in the life of our Lord did His mother drink of His cup of agony. Her first dolor began with His infancy, and lasted all His life. But it was not only the view of the nail, and the spear, and the cross, which overwhelmed her; she had ever before her the thought of His rejection and its consequences. She entered into the desolation of His soul at the ingratitude of mankind. So much condescension, so much love, so much suffering, was to be wasted upon an ungrateful world. The chosen nation, descendants of Abraham, Isaac, and Jacob, were to reject the Messiah and to crucify their God. His blood was to be upon them and their children for ever, and they were to be outcasts from the promises of their fathers. So many souls were to be redeemed, and so few to be finally saved!

It is impossible for us to know all the sorrow which this prophecy of St. Simeon poured upon the pure soul of the Blessed Virgin. For she had long enjoyed the vision of God, and hence could endure a grief which would have been too great for an ordinary human life. Yet two considerations force themselves upon us—the share we have had in her suffering, and the contrast between her sorrow and our own. The exalted dignity of Mother of God brought the Blessed Virgin into the direct counsels of God, and gave her an especial place in the economy of redemption. As suffering was the great means by which the Son was to expiate the sins of the world, so the mother was forced to take her share in the sacrifice. As, then, our sins have caused the passion and death of our Lord, so have they caused the sorrow of His mother. Our sinful thoughts, our transgressions of word and action, were the arrows which pierced the mother's soul while they wounded the heart of the Son. We sinners have had our share in the passion of the sinless Virgin. If then, we receive grace to compassionate her woes, we ought to lament the work of our own hands, and seek through her prayers a perfect purification from the sins by which we made ourselves instruments of her agonies. Mother of sorrows as she is, her heart is ever open to the penitent, and her hands are always stretched out to the afflicted.

And no one, who has lived even a short time in this world, has been without his experience of sorrow. We are born exiles from Paradise our true home, and the victims of the penalties of original and actual sin. When we suffer, we reap the harvest our own hands have sown. And, no matter to what afflictions the providence of God calls us, we know we can never endure what our sins deserve. We too, have before us a foreboding of evil, and a fear of the divine judgments. But it is conscience that plants this thorn in our hearts. The Blessed Virgin suffered sinless, and on account of her intimate union with our Lord. We suffer full of sins, and on account of our estrangement from our merciful Redeemer. There is this one consolation to the sufferer. If he accept joyfully his cross and endure with patience, he is following in the steps of Jesus and Mary. Sorrow will efface the debt he owes to the divine justice. It will wash away the defilement of past sin. It will bid the world and sense retire, and will open the soul to the operations of the Holy Spirit. The passion of the Blessed Virgin was an integral part in the work of her great sanctification. It brought her under the cross, and daily nearer and nearer to God. So may our afflictions be the means of detaching us from things sensible, and fastening our affections to Him who alone is good and beautiful and true. Days of wholesome fear are, for us sinners, days of God's most merciful visitation.

CHAPTER X.

THE FLIGHT INTO EGYPT—DAY OF SELF-SACRIFICE.

"Flee away, O my Beloved, and be like to the roe, or to the young hart upon the mountains of aromatical spices."—CANTICLES, viii. 14.

Our Blessed Lord was rejected by man even before His birth, and was born in a stab e. He first opened His eyes upon poverty, and the contempt of the world He had created. Yet now we are to see the hand of violence raised to insult His sacred person, and to destroy if possible His infant life. Herod, the king of Judea, heard of the coming of the Messiah, who was by prophecy to be king of the Jews. The Magi from the East had been to his court, telling of the miracle which had led them to seek His cradle. Fearing therefore for his own temporal power, he resolved to find out the abode of our Lord, that under the pretence of adoring Him, he might take His life. As the hour for the sacrifice was not come, the child Jesus was forced to flee from the persecution, and to be an exile from His own country. The angel of the Lord appeared to St. Joseph by night, and bade him arise and take the young child and His mother and fly into Egypt. So in the dead of night, without any preparation for the journey, the holy family arose and escaped from the land of Juda. The tender Virgin of only fifteen years takes her infant in her arms, and under the guidance of St. Joseph, begins her long pilgrimage. They were forced to travel through deserts and over mountains, exposed to all the hardships of the forest, for four hundred miles, until they reached the land of bondage, out of which God had by wonderful miracles delivered the whole Jewish nation. More than once were they almost famished for food, and in the terrors of the wilderness were exposed to the attack of wild beasts, or the more merciless assassin. From these dangers the angels of God often rescued them. But what a sight, to see the Lord of Heaven and His Mother in these hardships! Wearied and exhausted, they found no place to lay their heads at night, save under the shelter of the forest-tree, or on the rocks of the wilderness. Jesus slept on Mary's bosom, and when Mary sank exhausted to sleep, St. Joseph kept vigil around their rude couch. After a journey of more than thirty days, they reached the land of Egypt, a land of idolatry, and found none to welcome the coming of the Son of God. There are traditions which tell us how the voice of inanimate nature proclaimed the presence of its king, and how the idols in the temples fell on their faces before the true God. Here, in a country where the religion of the patriarchs was unknown, St. Joseph sought a shelter for the Virgin and her child, and here in poverty and distress for seven years they abode. They had no need to turn their faces towards Jerusalem, as the captive Israelites had done, for the glory of the holy city had departed. The pillar of fire, the ark of God, the manna from Heaven, the glory which abode between the Cherubim was exiled in the land of the pagan. In estimating the sorrows of Mary, we can consider her own physical distress during this long journey and still longer exile. The bodily fatigue and privation were no small trial of her tender frame. Yet this is but the smallest part of her dolor. It was her mother's heart which was made to bleed. The hardships through which her child was forced to pass, and the ignominy heaped upon Him, broke up the very depths of sorrow in her heart. A little infant is driven from home at night and forced to flee from the sword of a jealous king, and the martyred innocents are sent up to Heaven as mementoes of His childhood. All Judea is armed against Him to drive Him into the wilderness, to shut out from His eyes the light which He created, and to starve him with hunger and thirst. And Mary, all the while adoring Him as the God of her salvation, felt every indignity which He so meekly and uncomplainingly received. To her the desert with Him in her arms was better than all Heaven without Him. But the more she knew of His love and grace, the more she felt the world's ingratitude. And this was but the beginning of the melancholy end. The life which the sword of Herod could not reach, was to expire on the cross. All these things and many more than we can know, passed before the afflicted soul of our Mother of Sorrows. As God alone has a true hatred of our sin, so God alone could properly estimate the injury thus offered to Himself. But Mary, looking always into His perfections, and herself an agent in the work of redemption, was able to enter into even the divine view of sin, and to grieve as no other creature can grieve at man's ingratitude. Nor did her grief ever disturb for one instant the serenity of her soul. Her sorrow was too deep and too divine for any outward manifestation. God's providence enveloped her. A tranquil, steady grief grew and matured itself in her heart, a grief which came from God and was all for Him, for she was wrapped in the same mantle which covered her child. So early began the work of expiation, and the new-born infant touched the cross with His tiny hands, and the mother was forced to cry out: "Flee away, O my Beloved, and be like to the roe, or to the young hart upon the mountains of aromatical spices." Go in thy infant years, and be an exile from thine own people upon the high mountains of sorrow, where Thy brethren have prepared for Thee wormwood and gall for thy food, and myrrh for thy sepulchre. In contemplating this dolor of the Blessed Virgin, we are at once struck with remorse at the similarity between our conduct and that of the Jews. How often have we been favored with the visit of Jesus and Mary, and how often have we repulsed their embraces? They have come to us to detach us from earthly things and to sanctify us. We have preferred the pleasures of the world and the gratification of our own wills, and were unwilling to stay in their company. Hence we have driven them from our hearts, or by the hand of mortal sin have persecuted them beyond our borders. No ingratitude of man was ever worse than this, for the sinful Jew had never been washed in the blood of Calvary, or born again of water and the Holy Ghost. We have done despite to the Spirit of grace, and have banished the Son of God from our hearts. Yet now once more the Mother comes with her child, knocking at the door of our hearts. If we receive her now, the past shall be all forgotten, and in the mercies of this season we shall find strength to open our hearts to God, that He may take full possession of our souls and abide with us forever. And if thus with true hearts we seek the Lord and Him alone, we must be content to take our share in His exile. The world will become our enemy, and we shall be forced to flee like Jesus and Mary, and God will enable us to enter into their spirit of self-sacrifice. Over hill and mountain, in unfrequented places, amid the terrors of evil spirits, the path of our perfection shall lead us, until the flesh loses its charm, and God becomes the supreme rest of our souls. Let us never fear. We leave the world and its darkness behind us. We go with Jesus and Mary, and with them we shall find Heaven and eternal peace. Let us cherish then the darkness through which the unfading light will one day shine. Let us remember that we are pilgrims and exiles journeying home. For are we not by baptism fellow-citizens of the saints, and members of the household of God? By this spirit of self-sacrifice let us judge ever of our spiritual state. We draw near to God in proportion as we forsake the world and the things of sense. When this earth becomes in reality a desert to us, through longing for God's presence, then in this wilderness we shall travel with Jesus and Mary and Joseph and all the saints.

CHAPTER XI.

THE LOSS OF JESUS IN THE TEMPLE—DAY OF LONELINESS.

"I opened the bolt of my door to my Beloved: but He had turned aside and was gone. My soul melted when He spoke. I sought Him and found Him not: I called, and He did not answer me."—CANTICLES, v. 6.

AFTER a sojourn of several years in Egypt, the holy family returned to Nazareth, and Jesus remained in childlike subjection to His mother. Who can tell the days of grace which were spent in that holy house, where the incarnate Lord daily grew in wisdom and stature, every hour manifesting through His growing body more and more of the power of deity? This life of prayer and praise was varied only by the observance of the duties of religion. Every year they went up to the temple at Jerusalem to keep the great paschal festival. And

when our Lord was twelve years old, they went up, according to the custom of the feast, and having fulfilled the days, they returned home. The child Jesus, however, remained in the temple, and, amid the immense concourse, his parents, for the first hour of their journey, missed Him not, but "supposed Him to be in the company among their kinsfolk and acquaintance." They therefore journeyed home, and not finding Him, were plunged in the deepest distress. They retraced their steps to Jerusalem, seeking Him everywhere along the road, until after three days they found Him in the temple, "sitting in the midst of the doctors, hearing them and asking them questions. And seeing Him they wondered. And His mother said to Him, Son, why hast Thou done so to us? Behold, Thy father and I have sought Thee sorrowing. And He said to them, how is it that you sought Me? Did you not know that I must be about my Father's business?"*
This dolor of our Blessed Lady consisted in

* St. Luke, ii. 41—51.

the temporary loss of Jesus, and is full of mystery. It was, perhaps, the greatest of all Mary's sorrows, while it is the most difficult to be understood First of all, there could be no grief to her like the loss of her child. All else to her was as nothing. She had all a mother's love for an only child, heightened to a degree of which we can form no just conception. United to her maternal affection was the supreme adoration of her soul. He was her child, her God, and her all. Suddenly He withdrew Himself from her, and with the loss of His presence He allowed the curtains of fear and gloom to be drawn around the happy heart of His mother. He gave her no idea of His purpose ; He made no explantions. He even withdrew His own inward consolations, and sent her away without Him to a cold and ungrateful world. So the poor and desolate mother was bereaved indeed. All nature lost its beauty in her eyes. The holy house at Nazareth, with so many mementoes of Him, was only an aggravation of her grief. "Tears were her bread day and night, while it was daily said to her, where is thy God?" In all that she had seen before, the ways of providence were clear. In this there was an impenetrable darkness, and she was plunged into something of that deep abjection which led her Son to cry out on the cross, "My God, My God, why hast Thou forsaken Me." In all her other dolors Jesus was with her, even when His torn hands and bleeding side broke her heart. Here she was alone. Her Beloved "had turned aside and was gone. She sought Him and found Him not: she called, and He did not answer her." Three days of this grief were like many years, and left the imprint of sorrow upon her beautiful frame. There was no food for her but the bread of tears, no sleep amid the vigils of a breaking heart. And in this gloom which overshadowed her she found a wilderness darker than the forests of Egypt. The tempter, whose head she had crushed, could only wait around the portals of the tabernacle which God had sanctified for Himself. Yet with all his malignity, he wished to bring new clouds of fear around the home he could not enter. He saw the Virgin sorrowing and alone. Her child had deserted her. What was the end of this separation? Had the sinless mother given any offence to her Beloved? She could not say she had not loved Him, for every fibre of her heart was His, and yet perhaps she had not served Him as she ought. She was only the handmaid of the Lord. She was unworthy to be His mother. Was her life only a bright dream of heaven? Was she no more to see that face, or live in His smile again? Had she proved unfaithful to her celestial spouse, and had He deserted her for ever? As we know not the joy of the Mother of God, nor the bliss of her daily communion with Jesus, so we cannot understand the misery of her loss. St. Simeon had told her of the cross, and she saw no cross on the height of Calvary. The hour was not come, and this was not the cross. It was a depth of woe she could not have anticipated, for it was like the displeasure of her Beloved, and this would have chilled the current of her life. So the sorrowing mother wept, and her sighs went up to the throne of her Son. She was going through the valley of darkness to seek and find a nearness to God which even she had not before known. Her child had not deserted her; He had hid His face through His great love. She was drinking of the torrent in the way, that she might lift up her head amid the sorrows of Calvary, when all flesh should fail, and at last upon God's holy mountain for ever. So in firm trust and unfailing hope she drank her cup of agony, and asked nothing but to see the face of her Son in His own good time. From this great and mysterious dolor of the Blessed Virgin we may learn submission to the ways of divine providence, and especially in the higher walks of the spiritual life. No one can come near our Lord without in some way touching His cross. Affliction in some form is our natural lot, since we are all born in sin, and inheritors of death. Desolation of heart is not only the consequence of our fallen state, but also a most important mean of sanctification. Youth is enthusiastic, and manhood is impetuous, and old age is selfish. It is only by affliction and self-denial that we learn how deceitful are the promises of the world, and how untrue is every thing earthly. Religion renders this natural experience conducive to the purification of our souls, and even makes loneliness of heart, which the unregenerate soul dreads, a merciful visitation of God. And, perhaps, there is no other way of subduing worldliness, which infests even the most chosen hearts, and from whose invasions no sacred asylum is free. To live for the world, even under its most innocent aspect, is not the end of our being. To regard its maxims, or to be governed by its influence, is a grievous infirmity fatal to all true spiritual life. The way of the cross is in some way the path of every good christian. And if God should lead any of us into great spiritual darkness, and seem to withdraw His presence from us, let us imitate the faith and patience of Mary. God would render us more worthy of that bright light for which He reserves us, and in the night, which is sure to bring a glorious day, we can be content. Constant self-examination, and dissatisfaction with our own hearts will bring humility and abasement, which lead to exaltation. We sinners ought, therefore, never to dread loneliness, or even gloom, which has in it no element of discouragement. Beautiful is the night, in which at least, God puts all the shadows of sense to flight. If with pure hearts we seek Him for His own sake, and seek Him patiently, knowing that we are unworthy to find Him, He will, in His good time, manifest Himself to us. Let us cherish whatever draws our affections away from things earthly. The heart, that is lonely and desolate through love of God, will certainly be filled with joy, when amid the darkness either of our own sins, or of His jealous chastisement, Jesus appears to take us to His embrace for ever.

CHAPTER XII.

THE MEETING OF JESUS AND MARY ON THE WAY TO THE CROSS—DAY OF GRIEF.

"The voice of my Beloved, knocking: Open to me, my sister, my love, my dove, my undefiled, for my head is full of dew, and my locks of the drops of the night."—CANT. v. 2.

AFTER the sorrow we have considered in the preceding chapter, our Blessed Lord returned home with His mother and was subject to her, as a child. There ensued from this hour a long period of comparative peace and tranquility to the Blessed Virgin. The holy house at Nazareth was like an outer court of Heaven, where Jesus, Mary, and Joseph lived in humility and poverty. The Holy Ghost has not revealed the scenes that transpired in that happy home. There our Lord gave us the example of all heroic virtues, submitting to every hardship, and laboring with His own hands to aid St. Joseph and to support His mother. Yet no one could be near Him and not partake of His spirit, and hence from every word, and look, and feature, the holy Virgin daily drank in godlike lessons of wisdom and conformity with her Son. There can be no doubt that the approaching passion was often the subject of converse, and Mary was taught her part in the great drama of blood. The meaning of the law and the prophets became daily more manifest to her, and the ways of divine providence were illuminated. The hour of separation approached, and then, for the brief space of His ministry, she was to be alone, interceding with God, and waiting for the great hour when all should be consummated. But before the hour of loneliness, St. Joseph, the last of the patriarchs, on whom she had so long leaned, was taken to his rest. The death of this great saint was like his life. He expired peacefully, with his head pillowed upon the bosom of Jesus, and with Mary kneeling at his side. As his life was the example of every virtue, so his departure was the pattern of a christian death, which the Holy Ghost calls a sleep in Jesus. The voice of St. John the Baptist now sounded in the wilderness, "Prepare ye the way of the Lord, make His paths straight." This was the knell which told of her separation, and in a few months the Son of God left His mother to begin His ministry among the Jews. The Virgin was left alone. Yet with a mother's anxiety she watched the daily report of His wonderful works. She heard of His words to the multitude, of His miracles, of His daily toil, when He had no place to lay His head, save in the wilderness, where His nights were spent in prayer. From His baptism in Jordan, and His wonderful fast in the desert, she followed His course to the last and final rejection by her own nation. The Jews had often sought His life, but they had no power, for the hour was not come. But now the mother knew that the hour was at hand, and she waited in fear and distress for the end. He went out in the evening to the garden of Gethsemane, and there the traitor found Him. One of the disciples ran from that scene to tell His mother how a fearful agony and a sweat of blood had overwhelmed Him. In that weak state Judas found opportunity to betray Him with a kiss. The mother heard how they threw Him on the ground and bound His hands, and fastening a heavy rope around His waist, dragged Him across the streets of Jerusalem to the palace of the high priest. She heard of the insults and tortures of that long night. The morning came at last, and she watched for the coming of the beloved disciple. He had stood by our Lord the whole night. He had followed Him to the court of Pilate. That unjust judge had pronounced Him innocent, and yet had exposed Him to all the fury of His enemies. St. John told the sorrowing Virgin of that awful and unheard-of scourging, which was far too much for any human tongue to describe. And then, to crown all, Pilate had given order for His crucifixion. The leaders of the people already had the sentence in their hands, and, in the midst of an insulting multitude, they were dragging Him to Mount Calvary. The Mother of sorrows saw now that her hour had come, and she nerved herself for her work. She would go out with St. John, she would see her Son, she would stand by His cross, she would stand by Him to the last. No sooner had they emerged from the house where she was lodging, than she heard the sound of the trumpet proclaiming Pilate's sentence. From a distance came up the shouts of the mob, and the cry, "crucify Him, crucify Him," rang in her ears. They hastened their footsteps until they came in sight of the procession. The mob came rushing by with violence, but Mary stood firm, unmindful of their imprecations, until she should see her Son. And O! what a sight for a mother to look upon. He had been almost deformed by the tortures of the night, the lashes of the scourge, and the insults of the multitude. His flesh was all torn off His back, and the blood was running down to His feet and moistening the pavement at every step He was walking to Calvary in His own blood. His head wore a crown of thorns, which were pressing down into the substance of His brain, and on His mangled shoulders He bore the two great heavy beams of His cross. Around His waist they had bound a thick rope, and the shouting rabble were dragging Him along. More than once He had fainted under the load, but His cruel tormentors had no mercy. Here His afflicted mother met Him. She called Him by His precious name. They had not met for many months. He heard her voice and turned to look upon her, wiping the clotted blood from His eyes, that He might return her compassionate love. Her woe added a new pang to His already broken heart. She rushed to touch Him, to do something of a mother's office to His bleeding wounds. But the soldiers rudely seized her, and threw her back upon the ground, and the crowd pressed on, and the mournful mother was forced to follow at a distance. With St.

John she followed in the steps of her Son's blood, adoring every moment the great price of redemption.

This dolor of our Blessed Lady is too great a depth for us to fathom. No one but Jesus then knew the immensity of her woe. She suffered in her own heart, she suffered in His heart. She felt all His wounds, and grief full and fervent filled every faculty of her soul. The past, present, and future were blended together. Never from her eyes could the image of sorrow fade away; never could she forget the look of love which He gave her when His eyes were weeping blood. This was her beautiful one, chief among ten thousand, and now He was deformed more than man, and His form than the sons of men. And so the Virgin's tears were mingled with the blood of Jesus in this great day of expiation.

Here, then, is a place for the sinner to weep. Countless sins have opened all these wounds, and here the ungrateful soul may weep at its own work. There is a time when the fountain of tears should be unlocked, when deep sorrow may atone for deep ingratitude. When the wounds of Jesus are all open, it is time for the sinner's wounds to be open too. Tears of contrition will fertilize the barren heart, and give new life to the dying soul. Let us weep to-day with our afflicted mother. Grief for her sorrows and for our transgressions will be acceptable incense in the sight of Heaven.

CHAPTER XIII.

THE DEATH OF JESUS—DAY OF REMORSE.

"Till the day break, and the shadows retire, I will go to the mountain of myrrh and to the hill of frankincence."— CANTICLES, iv. 6.

St. John and the Blessed Virgin followed the crowd, and made their way to the place of crucifixion. The course of the mob was arrested several times by the falling of our Lord under the heavy weight of the cross. After the seventh fall they were obliged to put the cross upon Simon of Cyrene, lest the victim should die before their vengeance was satiated. The Virgin heard all, and saw how her Son was fainting away, but she could not get near Him. At last they came to the ascent of Calvary, and on its brow they paused in the place of skulls, where unburied bodies had lain in corruption, and where the air was infected with noxious vapors. Here in a rock they made a place for the upright beam of the cross. They laid the wood upon the ground and made the transverse beam fast, and then with violence they threw Jesus down upon it. Mary heard Him fall, and knew they were laying Him out upon the cross. They stretched out His hands, dislocating all the joints of His arms, and then with heavy mallets they drove the nails through them. When His hands were fastened, they drew violently down His body, and with one long nail driven through both His feet, they completed the crucifixion. Mary heard the sound of the mallets, and every blow pierced her heart. She would have suffered less if the nails had been in her own flesh. The victim was now laid out upon His bed of pain, and the soldiers gathered a crowd to raise the cross. With cries and shouts of derision they bore the cross and its victim to the hole in the rock, and then with a terrible jolt they let it down into its place. This violent shock opened afresh every wound, and caused the saving Blood to gush out at every pore. They then took two malefactors and crucified them on either side, and with jeers and insults they continued to deride the meek and suffering Jesus. When they were somewhat satiated with these tortures, they withdrew a little, and the afflicted mother found opportunity to draw near the cross. The beloved disciple and Magdalen followed her, and they were unable to console themselves, still less to solace the heart of the Virgin. She came close up to our Lord and looked up into His face to assure Him of her sympathy. What a sight for a mother to look upon! The hands and feet of her Beloved were nailed, and on three dreadful wounds hung the whole weight of His body. The bones were all dislocated and almost forcing their way through the skin. The crown of thorns still pressed into His head, and He could not even rest it upon the cross, for at every motion some new thorn was forced into His brain. There the mother stood and trembled as the cross shook and quivered with the dying agonies of her Son. She could not alleviate His pangs. She could not ease his woe. And when through tears of blood He looked down to recognize her, He saw her broken heart and new grief overpowered Him. His gentle, His beautiful mother, she was suffering with Him. She was breaking down under the weight of His grief. Mary saw this and her eyes were cast down, and from that summit of Calvary she looked down upon Jerusalem and the world, and uniting her heart with her Son's, she offered the great sacrifice for man's salvation. Virtue such as no creature had dreamed of, such as no saint can conceive, crowned her holy obedience. God accepted her great sorrow and her perfect resignation. No human heart can enter into her woe. We can only describe faintly the externals of the scene; we cannot penetrate into the interior of her passion. Her sorrow stands out alone and unapproachable on the page of human woe. She drew near to the heart of her Son, and as far as creature could she shared in His mysterious agony. When three hours had passed and the sun was at high noon, suddenly he veiled his face, and great darkness covered the earth. A cold terror seized the multitude, and they shrank away with fear. The mother was left undisturbed at the foot of the cross, as the priest stands in silence and solemn awe before the dread altar. Four times had our Lord spoken— once to pray for the pardon of his murderers, once to forgive the penitent thief, once to express his fearful thirst and to fulfil the prophecy by taking their cup of vinegar and gall; once before the whole universe to recognize His mother, and to bequeath her to us in the words, "Son, behold thy mother." Now a new darkness comes over His soul. He withdraws from Himself the consolations of His divinity, and in the fearful agony which ensues, cries out with a loud voice, "My God, My God, why hast Thou forsaken Me!" This was the height of His passion, and its most mysterious depth. The accents of this cry shook the feeble frame of Mary, and almost caused her death. She trembled like the tree shaken by the gale, or the bark shivered by the storm, and clung to the cross for support in that awful moment. There she stood, clasping with both arms that cross which was now shaking with the last convulsions of her dying Son. The angel of death hovered near. He heard his Creator say, "Into Thy hands, O Father, I commend My Spirit." His pinions touched the cross. One word more, "It is consummated," and Jesus was dead—and Mary looked up once more, a widowed, childless mother. Who should give her comfort now? The light of Heaven was put out. The world had killed its Redeemer. She had lost her Son. The earth, which was Heaven with Him, was now a dreary desert, and she was alone.

Yet more than martyr, without even the consolations of Him, for whom and with whom she suffered, she stood firmly beneath His cross. The sword of Simeon pierced through her heart, and to God she offered her pain. It was her part in the world's redemption.

Here, then, let the sinner pause and contemplate the cost of his salvation. Let him mark well every step in this mysterious passion, and by all its infinite value, learn the price of his own soul and the malignity of his sins. Our sins of hand, and foot, and tongue were the nails which fastened our Lord to the cross. Our persevering ingratitude pursued Him even to death and oppressed His dying breath. Let us give way to remorse for what we have done, for what perhaps we are doing now. The past cannot be undone. Its burden of sin must be brought to Calvary, and the soul defiled must there be washed once more, or God can never be our portion. Let us bring our guilty selves to the bar of conscience, and there find ourselves guilty of the death of Christ, and only seek the mercy He proclaimed to the penitent thief. The prayers of the Mother of sorrows shall be our refuge, if with true hearts we sympathize in her grief. And when we approach the valley of the shadow of death, Mary will be with us, and in death, as a just and willing punishment for sin, we shall find the entrance to eternal peace. Where Jesus and Mary are, there shall be no darkness, for the sting of death is taken away, and the narrow portals of the grave have lost their gloom. Shall the sinner fear to tread in the road which was hallowed by the footsteps of his God?

CHAPTER XIV.

THE PIERCING OF THE SIDE OF OUR LORD—DAY OF GRATITUDE.

"The stream of the river maketh the city of God joyful. The Most High hath sanctified His own tabernacle."—Psalm, xlv. 5.

THE Blessed Virgin remained standing at the foot of the cross, supported by her sister, Mary the wife of Cleophas, by the Magdalen, and the beloved disciple. There they stood in speechless woe, while darkness covered the whole earth and all nature seemed convulsed with grief. No sooner had our Lord spoken His expiring word, that at once an earthquake shook the whole city, sending terror into every heart and opening the graves of many of the elder saints. A funeral pall was spread over the nation that had shed the blood of its God.

The centurion who kept guard, when he saw all these portents, exclaimed, "truly this was the Son of God." Yet no sympathy came to the afflicted mother. Her sorrow was too deep for human consolation. She stood riveted to the cross, broken-hearted and desolate. At last in the distance is heard the sound of a multitude. They are groping their way in the darkness, to see if their victims are already dead. The morrow was the great day of the passover, and these bodies must be removed before the dawn. The two thieves are not yet dead; they are writhing in their last agonies. So with violence they draw near, and the soldiers take great mallets to break their legs. They soon dispatch these poor victims, and coming to the cross of our Lord, they find Him already departed. There was no need to break His legs, but a Roman soldier mounted, comes up with a long spear and pierces His heart. At once there flows from that sacred heart a mingled tide of water and blood. It was a miraculous torrent gushing from the sacred body full of love for the guilty sons of men, and of power to wash away every stain and defilement. St. John, who saw it, bears witness to it, as to one of the great facts of revelation. "And he that saw it gave testimony, and he knoweth that his testimony is true."* If mothers watch with jealous care the remains of their children, lingering in fond affection over the last that is left to them, much more did Mary burn with love and zeal for the honor of that torn and mangled body. It was the body of her child, dearer to her than her own flesh and blood. It was the body of her God, from which, in all its ignominy, the deity never for a moment departed. Ten thousand angels were veiling their faces before its bleeding wounds, and Mary, purer, dearer than all, sent up every moment her supremest adoration. What horror must then have seized her to witness this new insult! It was a new and needless aggravation of her woe. Yet it was the accomplishment of a great prophecy, the manifestation of

* St. John, xix. 35.

God's great love for sinners, and the opening of the fountain for sin and uncleanness. It was the gushing of the stream of the river which makes glad the city of God. The sacred heart had overflown with mercy for a guilty world, and had broken with man's ingratitude. Now by the rude hand of violence its pulsations were stilled, and yet in death it yearned to give some new token of its pity for the fallen. The Roman spear comes to its aid, and the saving, cleansing stream flows out. Here is the beginning of all life and salvation. For the sinner can never draw nigh to God covered with the defilement of his sins. He must first be purified, and there is no earthly power which can wash him clean. The blood of Christ alone can cleanse him. This mingled tide of water and blood from the side of our Lord can purge the deepest stains, and this alone is the sinner's hope. The sacred heart was the place of Mary's rest, and into its depths of love she looked and found consolation. That last wound had well-nigh drawn with its bloody spear the current of her life. Two hearts were lacerated with that fearful blow. Still conscious of man's great joy, Mary looks on in the future to the choir of saints who should wash their robes and make them white in the blood of the Lamb. She sees the church of God coming like our mother Eve, from that open side, and living in its fonntain of sanctifying grace. The spouse of the second Adam is born upon the cross, while He is wrapped in His sleep of death. And she too looked up with gratitude for that crimson flood, though it cost the sacrifice of her own heart.

And now the shades of evening began to thicken around Mount Calvary, and the holy women gather closer to the cross. Joseph of Arimathea, a just man and a counsellor, goes to Pilate, and begs in his own name and in Mary's behalf, for the body of Jesus. Pilate consents and gives the order. So another Joseph takes the place of the holy spouse of the Virgin, and comes with some of the disciples to prepare our Lord for burial. With reverence and awe they make ready to take the body from the cross. First they place long ladders against the cross, and draw out the long nails from the hands and feet. Then with care they gently bear the body in their arms and lift it to the ground. The Mother of sorrows waits to receive it, and they place the pale and bloodless head upon her bosom. She takes once more her Beloved into her arms, and the disciples kneel around her to adore the Word made flesh. Magdalen embraces His feet and again washes them with her tears, while the holy Virgin kisses each wound and wipes away the clotted blood. She closes His eyes and composes His sacred features. All was obedient to her touch, save the outstretched arms which could not be closed, but remained open to welcome to His embrace the sinners for whom He died. Here for some moments in silence they waited, not daring to intrude upon Mary's grief. But what a sight for men and angels! The Mother of God sits at the foot of the cross, and holds in her arms the body of her dead Son, while tears stream down from her face, mingling with the blood still issuing from His wounds. To this sight, before which the angelic army is mute with grief, let the sinner turn. It is the day of his recovery. Let him bring his sorrows and his miseries here. Though his sins be like crimson, they shall be white as wool. Here is the Jordan in which the unclean and leprous may put off their defilements, and regain the flesh and the heart of an innocent child.

CHAPTER XV.

THE BURIAL OF JESUS—DAY OF ABASEMENT.

"My dove in the clefts of the rock, in the hollow places of the wall, show me thy face, let thy voice sound in my ears; for thy voice is sweet and thy face comely."—CANTICLES, ii. 14.

AFTER the holy women kneeling around the Mother of sorrows had adored for some time the body of Jesus, they begin the preparations for His burial. Joseph of Arimathea has a new tomb hewn in a rock quite near to Calvary, and here he has made ready a place for his God. They wrap the body in fine linen and anoint it with the choicest spices. It is now quite dark, and the rabble, tired and alarmed, have gone home, and there is no fear of intrusion. The funeral procession starts from the mount. Joseph and the disciples bear the holy body in their arms; the beloved

St. John acts his part of son, and supports the Virgin, while the holy women follow mournfully behind. The childless mother's thoughts are full of bitter woe. As she walks behind the dead body of her Son, memory peoples her mind with a thousand sad recollections. She goes down the ascent by which in the morning she came up following the track of the precious blood. All the events of that long day one by one return to her. It seemed as if she had lived a century in that one day, so fast had come the accelerations of her woe. Now it was over and all was still as death. They reach the sepulchre and pause a moment before its open door. Then gently they lay Jesus to His rest upon that bed of stone. They kneel around the tomb while Mary goes in to take a last look of her child. They have hidden her dove in the clefts of the rock, but no voice sounds in her ears, and the face is cold in death. Yet it is the Resurrection and the Life whom they leave shut up in the hollow place of the wall. It is the unchangeable nature of God which lies imprisoned in that sepulchre. They roll the stone to the door and prepare to take their departure. A band of Roman soldiers come to take their place, not indeed to adore the Lord of life, but to guard His tomb. The holy mother goes to her house supported by St. John, for home now on earth she had none. Magdalen and the holy women retire to a little distance, and sit down to watch the sepulchre. Most of us have in some way known affliction, and can tell by experience of the bitterness of bereavement, and how it casts a shadow over all earthly things. The very sun in heaven loses its brightness and the elasticity of hope seems to desert us. The long nights seem to have no morning, and the weary days no evening. Far worse than all this was Mary's affliction. She had lost her life and light, her child and her God, and she had lost Him by the most cruel and ignominous of deaths. Now He was in the grave, in the likeness of corruption, and she was on earth alone. In this almost endless night of sorrow every thing comes back to her. She recalls the transports of Bethlehem when first in the manger she kissed His lips a thousand times and called Him her own. She remembers the long journey into Egypt, and how its hardships wore upon His tender frame. She brought before her mind all the endearments of the holy house at Nazareth, and the numberless winning ways of His childhood. She tries to picture His looks of affection by which so often He had poured into her soul new grace and new bliss. And of late she had thrown on Him the whole weight of her heart, and had kept neither care nor anxiety for the future. Then every step of the passion comes before her again. She sees Him bleeding under the scourge, fainting under the cross, and looking love to her even in the agonies of death. And in the vigils of that night she is ever before the sepulchre, now lying down by His side on His stony bed, now trying in vain to roll away the rock from the entrance, or frightened away by the tramp of the Roman soldier. Poor mother, there is no one who can sympathize with her woe, and no one but God could read the utter desolation of her heart. That tomb is her burial place also, and in it she is shut up, and by it she is cut off from all the things of earth. She shall indeed rise with her Son to new life and glory, but these are the days of her burial. He who would rise with Christ must first die with Him and be buried with Him. The Blessed Virgin was the first to follow the example of her Son, for from Him she was never separated. As she revealed to St. Bridget, the spear that pierced His heart pierced hers also, the tomb that enclosed His body was also her resting-place. There was no need that she should die to the things of sense; they had never found entrance in her heart. There was no need that she should be buried to the world, for she had never known the world or felt even one of its attractions. There was no purgative life for her. Yet in the high and majestic union of her soul with God there were continually new heights and ever deeper depths. And her share in the cross and passion was one of the fruits of this union. The sinner however, as he contemplates Mary's grief, and beholds his Lord sleeping in the embrace of death, may find many lessons leading him to compunction and self-abasement. That cold tomb encloses the hearts both of Jesus and Mary. Let the sinner kneel before it, and learn how to die and how to await resurrection.

For soon we must say to corruption, thou art my mother, and to the worm, thou art my sister, and soon we must sleep in the narrow grave, not in the likeness, but in the reality of corruption. Shall our long sleep be like the sleep of Jesus? Shall our tomb be like His? If such shall be our peaceful rest, then must we die with Christ to all things sensible, even to the desires of our own hearts. Then in humility and self-abnegation must we cut every chain that binds us to the world, and bid the stony door of His sepulchre shut out all else but Him and our own soul. Our world of faith shall be there where He is, and living on earth, we shall be indeed strangers and pilgrims, citizens of a better country. O blessed burial, hope of the sinner, and earnest of everlasting union with God! O blessed sepulchre, where no deceitful shadow of sense, no empty vision of the world can disturb the peaceful rest of the soul! Who would not seek thy hallowed gloom, and in it find alone the only good and the only true? But if we aspire to such likeness to Jesus and His Mother, we shall need great courage and great fidelity to grace. There is scarcely any human heart in which in some way the world does not reign. Worldliness is the great sin of our day, and like a devouring worm it eats at the root of every fair tree in the garden of God. We are ever striving to accomplish by human means what the divine providence would bring to pass in His own way. We ever turn out of the path of our perfection to try some easier way which presents some apparent gain; and in the perplexities of life, or in the blessed visitations of divine love, we turn to the creature and turn away from the Creator. The mystical death is not to be found except in the steep and narrow way, and the sepulchre of Jesus will not receive us till the world and its maxims, and its sensuality are utterly banished from our hearts. For in that narrow tomb no earthly thought can enter, and no heart can sleep there whose every pulsation is not for Jesus and Mary. Let us abase ourselves for our past neglect! Have we ever counted the cost, when for any earthly good we are sacrificing the favor of God, or throwing away even one grace which would lead us heavenward? Why have things sensible the power to dim the eye of faith, or to attract the soul that God would prepare for His own endless love and ravishing beauty? "Vanity of vanities, all is vanity." The cross of Christ is the measure of the world. The voiceless sepulchre is the mighty preacher of the nothingness of human promises. Why not seek that safe shelter from every storm and tempest, that shield from the defiling touch of everything earthly? The Mother of sorrows will be our teacher, and from her example we shall learn the way of self-abasement. She will be our guide through whatever paths God may lead us, and with her we cannot stray. And we shall make progress in our sanctification only in proportion as we walk in her footsteps, and conform our lives to the model she has given us. It will be a consolation to her afflicted heart to guide us to a perfect union with her Son, for whom she lived and suffered.

CHAPTER XVI.

THE RESURRECTION OF OUR LORD—DAY OF ILLUMINATION.

"The winter is now past, the rain is over and gone, the flowers have appeared, the time of pruning is come, the voice of the turtle is heard in our land."—CANTICLES, ii. 11—12.

THEY who sow in tears shall reap in joy. After a time of sorrow patiently endured for God, there comes a time of consolation and reward. The dolors of the Blessed Virgin were only her steps to endless glory when, after having suffered with Christ, she received power to arise and reign with Him. Following, therefore, the course of her holy life, we are to consider some of her glories, by which, before the whole universe, she obtained a reward for her virtues. The days of our Lord's passion were over. His sacred body rested in the sepulchre, guarded by Roman soldiers. His holy soul was in the chamber of the fathers, preaching to the spirits in prison, and preparing the saints of the old law for their triumphant entry into Heaven. A night, and a day, and a night intervened, and Mary kept watch for the accomplishment of His promise. Sleep never visited her eyes. She was waiting in anxious suspense for the third day. The great feast of the passover had lost its significance for her, for now the true paschal lamb had been sacrificed, and His flesh had been given for the life of the world. Figures and shadows had given place to the reality. The first morning watch of the third day found her on her way to the sepulchre. The whole city was buried in sleep, and even the holy women had not arisen, as they were waiting for the beginning of the dawn. She went alone in the darkness to anticipate the hour and to welcome her Son at His first rising. Her way led her over Mount Calvary. The crosses were still standing, and before them she knelt to adore the saving wood, still red with the blood of her Son. Then she goes towards the sepulchre, and patiently waits for the appointed hour. The guards are walking before the tomb, and Pilate's seal is still unbroken. All around her are the open graves which the earthquake at the death of Jesus had unclosed. These were the graves of many of the elder saints, for tradition tells us that our first father, Adam, and many of the patriarchs, were buried on this holy mountain. Here therefore, watched the Virgin Mother, recalling the past, meditating upon the plan of redemption, and tracing its course from man's fall through the promises made to the fathers, and the revelations given to the prophets. She was the queen of all those just souls who were now to find their perfection. While she is thus contemplating the adorable ways of God, suddenly the faintest tinge of light touches the eastern horizon, and instantly there is heard the rumbling of an earthquake. The whole city is shaken, and the rock is rolled away from the door of the sepulchre. The guards are alarmed, and look on with anxious fear, when suddenly through the open door our Lord appears surrounded with hosts of adoring angels. The soldiers fall upon their faces and become like dead men, and the heavenly army takes their place as keepers of the sepulchre. Jesus has put off the garments of corruption, and is clothed with incorruption. He has put off the ignominy of death, and has put on the vesture of eternal glory. His face is more dazzling than the sun, and His form more glistening than the brightest gems of earth. Mary looks up for Her share in this glory, and behold He runs to meet her, and once more folds her in His embrace. She looks once more upon His face, and never did His infant beauty seem so ravishing. She seeks for the glow of health, and behold the precious Blood flows again in its wonted channels, and the vigor of undying youth gleams in all His features. She looks at His wounds, and they are open still, but celestial light is beaming from them. A blissful ecstacy comes over her, and she seems to be in Heaven listening to the song of cherubim and seraphim, and hearing from her Son's lips the triumph of the resurrection. While thus she rejoices in the glory of Jesus, behold from the open graves ascend the bodies of them that slept in faith. They draw near the second Adam, and kneel at His feet. Prophets and kings now see Him whom they so long desired, and bear witness to the power of His victory over death. The soul of Mary is overwhelmed with light, and all the ways of redemption are now unveiled before her. Soon the bright vision vanishes, and Jesus guides His mother to her home at the house of St. John. He has yet to appear to Magdalen and the holy women, to Peter and the Apostles, who were to be witnesses of His resurrection. Yet who could tell the Virgin's part in the glory of that day! She was buried with her Son, and now she shares in His great victory. She rejoices to see the sacred Humanity clothed with its own proper glory, and to see the reward for all its ignominy. He who was so marred by the passion as to lose all form and comeliness, has now recovered his likeness to her, and shines with all the beauty of Heaven. This is her consolation, but this is not the beginning of her joy. She looks upon death and the grave, and sees that their terrors are gone. Beside the sepulchre lies the broken iron sceptre, and the crown of the enemy of man is shivered to pieces. She sees the resurrection of the just, in the likeness and in the glory of her Son. She looks upon the spiritual resurrection of souls, and sees how the dead in sin are to be quickened to new life by the power of this day. That open sepulchre is to her the entrance of Heaven, and the light which beams from it shines up to the gates of the celestial city. There is no more night for her. Her whole soul is illumined, and even she, in her perfection, makes a grand ascension towards God, and with her rising Son, draws nearer to the centre of all light and grace and bliss. The wounded heart is made whole, and the broken spirit is healed.

If we would participate in Mary's joy, we must, like her, wait upon the Lord, and like her be faithful in the day of trial. God waits to pour upon us His grace, and to fill us with His Spirit. If we would be illumined in every part, so that from us all darkness should flee away, then must we yield a ready obedience to that Spirit while He seeks to cast out of our souls all the dross of the old Adam, and to animate us with the power of the Resurrection and the Life. And if we would rise with Christ, then the attachments of earth must lose their power, and the spirit must be free to mount upward in the way which He has opened for us. Let us pray to the glorious mother to give us a part in the light of the Resurrection.

CHAPTER XVII.

THE ASCENSION OF OUR LORD—DAY OF JOY.

"Whither is thy Beloved gone, O thou most beautiful among women, whither is thy Beloved turned aside, and we will seek Him with thee."—CANTICLES, v., 17.

THE forty days which intervened between the resurrection and our Lord's ascension were days of light and grace to the Blessed Virgin. He was with His apostles, teaching them the things which pertained to the kingdom of God, and laying the foundations of His church. The holy mother was constantly at His side, and to her He opened the mysteries of revelation. If communion with Him had been full of bliss in the days of childhood and growing manhood, much more was it blissful now when man's redemption was purchased and He had put on the body of glory. Who can ever know, save Jesus and Mary, the hours of joy which during these forty days were her blessed reward for labor and suffering? Earth seemed to have receded in the far distance, and Heaven to have opened itself upon her transported soul. But labor was not over. The Virgin had still her work to do, as her hand was to be employed in the foundation of the church, and she was to enter upon her dominion as queen of the apostles. Our blessed Lord taught His mother the whole of His will, and guided her in the office to which she was appointed. He opened His whole heart to her, and left her for a few years on earth to be the support of His disciples. She was to be His representative in the perplexities of the infant church.

At last the time came when He was to leave the world and to ascend to His Father. Mary was to witness the glory and to participate in its blessedness. When the morning came He led her, accompanied by the apostles and many of His disciples, to the mount of Olives. There upon its summit He stood to take a last view of Jerusalem, and to bid farewell to His children. He knew how they would need His support, and how all should be baptized in His baptism of blood. He gave them his parting counsels and lifted up His hands to bless them. Suddenly a new radiance shone from all His features, a cloud of dazzling light enveloped Him, and swiftly, gently He was borne up out of their sight. His last look was upon His mother to cheer her in her bereavement and to nerve her for the work before her. He seemed to say, " Farewell dear Mother for a brief season only, I am going to prepare a bright throne for thee, and soon will send my angels to take thee, when thou like Me shalt be assumed in glory." Mary took the meaning of His look and gazed longingly after Him, till the bright clouds which curtained His ascent gathered into one, and naught was left but the majestic glories of the heavens, which caught the radiance of His departing form, and reflected back in purple, azure and gold the last beams of the light of the Son of Man. The Mother of God was again alone. For some moments the Apostles lingered gazing into heaven until the voices of angels reassured them of their master's farewell, and then they knelt around the stone on which were still imprinted the marks of His sacred feet. Then under the guidance of Mary they went back to the temple and began their great novena of prayer.—There are many considerations which go to make up the joy and glory of the Blessed Virgin in the triumphant ascension of her Son. It was indeed a temporary loss, and a long separation from the sight of Him whose face constituted her bliss. She was for some long years to be on earth alone, while He was to be enthroned in heaven. Her pilgrimage was not over and the dreary desert was still her portion. Yet He was now glorified and His sacred humanity had received its reward. His exaltation was her's also. Her heart now bound closer than ever to His, found rest with Him on the everlasting mountain. The way to heaven was opened for the soul and body of redeemed and regenerate man. And her child, her own flesh and blood, was crowned forever amid the burning glories of the eternal Trinity. Her child was sitting on the throne of God, His co-equal and consubstantial word. In Him therefore she was elevated and with Him she was glorified. He had ascended for the very purpose of drawing the human heart after Him, and she more than all others had merited the grace of this day. And as she stood looking after Him, her whole being went with Him, and from the dizzy hight of sanctity which she had reached, all human things were out of sight. She seemed to invite the salutation of the Canticles, " Whither O thou most beautiful among women, has thy Beloved gone, whither is thy Beloved turned aside, and we will seek Him with thee ?" And Mary was willing that her

Beloved should be gone, in order that she might induce us to seek Him with her. We have a right to participate in her joy, for the nature which ascended, and which sits at God's right hand, is our nature also. We have a part in this great exaltation. But then with mind and heart we must seek Him who is gone before us, and be citizens in truth of that better land to which He invites us "Who shall ascend into the mountain of the Lord, or who shall stand in His holy place? The innocent in hands and clean of heart."* The true way therefore to follow Christ, is to purify our hands and hearts from every stain of sin, and every affection to sin. We need to set always before our faces the sight of our ascended Lord, and to turn all our thoughts and affections to Him. We must open our souls to His attractions and let him draw us away from the things of time and sense. Thus we may make a true ascension every day, as we approach nearer to the divine model. This is the end of the grace of re-

* Psalm. xxiii. 3–4.

generation. It takes us away from our human generation and our human ties, and unites us to God by a truer bond. Mary was the mother of our Lord, and we are His children by a real participation in His nature. And as it is only by slow steps that this great ascension is accomplished, so we ought to ask for the aid of the Blessed Virgin that we may follow in the narrow way. Many make great progress and mount high upon the spiritual ladder, only to fall more fearfully by some great infidelity to God. Many lose the fruit of all their labors, when a little more perseverance would have gained for them an eternal crown. The heavens above us will not be always like those which curtained our Lord's ascent. We must go on in darkness as well as in light, and seek for none to know our hearts but God, nor ask for consolation from creatures. The ascending soul can never find such consolation. It is only a mockery of its great wants. He who reads our hearts and knows their sincerity will be our support, and even when clouds and darkness are round about Him, He is only bringing us closer to Himself, and preparing us for His infinite purity. He will never be separated from the soul that truly seeks Him.

CHAPTER XVIII.

THE COMING OF THE HOLY GHOST—DAY OF PEACE.

"The fountain of gardens, the well of living waters which run with a strong stream from Libanus. Arise, O north wind, and come. O south wind, blow through my garden, and let the aromatical spices thereof flow."—CANT. iv. 15-16.

WHEN our Lord had gone into heaven the apostles returned to Jerusalem, and spent their time at the temple in prayer. Mary returned with them, and under her guidance they passed their great novena. Ten days were given them to wait for the promise of the Holy Ghost. Mary interceded for them and with them that our

Lord would be mindful of His word, and send the powerful Paraclete upon them, who should more than make up for the loss of His visible presence. "It is expedient for you that I go away, said He, for if I go not away the Paraclete will not come to you; but if I depart I will send Him unto you." At Mary's feet they learned something of the meaning of this promise, and were daily in expectation of the great gift of the Father. During this short time the Mother of God presided in their councils, the number of the twelve apostles was filled up, and the foundations of the church were securely laid. When the tenth day had come they were assembled together in the temple, waiting for the completion of our Lord's promise. The great festival had called a vast multitude of Jews and proselytes from all Judea and the surrounding country. Great numbers were flocking to the temple from all parts of the city. The Mother of God and the twelve apostles were together in a small upper room, unknown and unnoticed amid the great throng of worshippers. Suddenly there was a sound as of a rushing, mighty wind. The temple trembled on its foundations. The Holy Ghost came down with might and power upon the disciples. First of all He crowned with light the holy Virgin, who was His own spouse, and then rested upon the apostles. Their faces were kindled with His glory, their whole bodies were lighted up with a heavenly radiance, and over their heads were cloven tongues of fire. The new creation had taken place. There was chaos no more in the moral world. The Spirit of God brooded upon the shapeless waters, and out of them came forth the church in life and beauty. The divisions of Babel were broken down, and the fold of Christ was opened to all the nations of the earth. The twelve were overwhelmed with the greatness of their vocation, as they saw the outlines of the kingdom over which they were to reign. Their eyes were opened, and the truths their Master had taught them were all made clear. They opened their mouths, and the gospel of Christ came full and fervent from their lips. The multitude crowded around to hear their words, and in every language they spake of the way of salvation through Christ. St. Peter began his work, and on that day more than three thousand were added to the flock. It was a day more wonderful than the day of the first creation, even as the spiritual life is more wonderful than the natural life. The Mother of God was glorified with these triumphs of the Holy Ghost. She received His consolations in her heart and she rejoiced at the new victories of her Son. To herself it was a day of peace. The blessed Paraclete, who had ever filled her heart and consecrated her whole being, now came to open to her new and new mysteries in the economy of salvation. She began to understand better than ever her own place in the work of redemption. The path through which she had come was illumined with the light of God's providence. She saw the full meaning of every word and work and look of her Son. All His labors and sorrows came back to her. The days of His blessed resurrection were before her mind, and every word which fell from His glorified lips seemed pregnant with wonderful power. She had ever bent adoringly before Him and had loved Him with the fullness of her heart. Now a new tenderness came over her, and she melted in an ecstacy of affection towards Him who was bone of her bone, and flesh of her flesh. A deep and quiet joy sank down to the depths of her spirit, and she could only repeat the words of her *Magnificat:* " My soul doth magnify the Lord, and my spirit hath rejoiced in God my Saviour." God had chosen her out of all the tribes of earth to be His mother. She had borne Him in her womb, had nourished Him at her breast, had been with Him in all His sorrows, had seen Him ascend into heaven. He was her own child. His interests were her's, and His glory was her's also. Her raptures on this day were the embraces of her own celestial spouse, and a peace passing all understanding filled every faculty of her spirit. God alone can tell what new graces were poured into her heart, for the dizzy height of sanctity on which she stood is far beyond the sight of sinners like us. "The well of living waters ran with a strong stream from Libanus." The Lord came into His own garden, and the aromatical spices thereof exhaled their perfume. But Mary also rejoiced at the wonderful works of the new creation. The church of God was born on this day, and the great energies of the sacraments began to put forth their strength. In Jerusalem was her rest, and in Zion her home. She was to exercise her office of Mother to all the spiritual children of her Son, and the nations were to be gathered to her feet. The triumphs of the church were her joy on this day, and the fruits of faith, which were to spring forth within it, were the consolation of her maternal heart. The Holy Ghost, who had made heaven so near to her, was now to dwell on earth, and to make its sterile plains a garden for the Lord of Hosts. In remembrance of this glory of the Blessed Virgin, we ought to lift up our hearts to a participation in her joy. We are her children, and her interests ought to be ours. Her work in our souls is our sanctification. She has no other care for us, and no temporal interests can divert her from this great work. If we have been obedient to the inspirations of the Holy Spirit we can share in her heavenly peace. Infidelity to God disturbs the tranquility of our souls, and makes us to wander in shadows and darkness. We are neither cheerful nor peaceful, only because we are continually hindering the work of grace. The Holy Ghost struggles against our wills, and cannot accomplish our sanctification. Mortal sin grieves the Comforter and drives Him away. Venial sin wounds Him, prevents the operation of His grace, and clogs the whole spiritual life. The flesh rises up with its stimulus of concupiscence, and passions unsubdued distract and divide our affections. We are anxious and fretful, only because the Spirit of peace is not our guide. Can we never find rest from warfare, and freedom from the persecutions of self-love?

"O wretched men that we are, who shall deliver us from this body of death?" Yes, rest will come when we have obtained perfect victory over passion. Peace will be ours when we yield our whole being to the guidance of the Holy Spirit. We are temples of the Holy Ghost, and the life of God is in us. That life is power by which sin and death may be utterly subdued. Let us only be obedient to God, and the divine life will produce its blessed fruits of peace. The embraces of the Paraclete will be an anticipation of heaven, and an imitation of the raptures of our holy Mother, whose unclouded eyes were always fixed upon the celestial glory And as we have been so often unfaithful, let us trust to the intercession of Mary to bring back to us the light of the Holy Spirit. Her prayers will be all-powerful with her spouse.

CHAPTER XIX.

THE DEATH OF THE BLESSED VIRGIN—DAY OF VICTORY.

"Stay me up with flowers, compass me about with apples, because I languish with love."—CANTICLES, ii. 5.

It was the will of God that the Blessed Virgin should linger on earth for a few years after the ascension of her Son. She had her part to perform in the foundation of the church, and she became the great consolation of the apostles in the absence of their Master. She who was wholly a sacrifice to God was willing to bear her exile when the interests of her Son required her presence on earth. Yet what a lonely exile was hers! Sometimes the saints have been raised above the attraction of earthly things to ardently long for heaven. They have found the world a bar ren desert, and the days of their pilgrimage long and wearisome. As the thirsty hart seeketh the stream of water, so their souls have been athirst for God. But what was their loneliness compared to that of the Mother of our Lord! Earth had long since vanished out of her sight. No human thing had any hold upon her. She was wholly absorbed in the love of her Son, and while He was with her she seemed to be in heaven also. Now he had left her, and the heart of the mother yearned unceasingly for her child. Her heart responded to the attractions of His heart, and its pulsations were still in unison with His. She could see His face no more. She could receive Him in the Blessed Eucharist, and be in spiritual communion with Him every moment, but His visible presence was no longer hers. The most dreary desert is not so drear to the exhausted traveler as was this world to her when Jesus had gone from it. In His Father's house were many mansions. He had gone to prepare a place for His children, and she knew of that bright throne which He was making ready for her. Yet the love He had shown her, and which He still manifested to her, only made her yearn the more for His presence. When should she be near Him again? When should she look into His face, and live in the light of His eyes? When should she once more embrace Him? His love was then her life, and as that love was ever increasing, it was one day to cause her death. Mary, being conceived without sin, had no part in the original curse. She was exempt from the pains and infirmities of mortality. The hand of disease never touched her beautiful form. She never grew old. She grew to perfect womanhood, and then she grew no more. Decay never laid his blighting finger upon her. She never suffered, except as she suffered for and with her Son. His passion had left its lines of anguish upon her fair brow, but none of the infirmities of man's fall came near her. Now she was to die, but not as ordinary mortals die. There was to be no wasting of nature, no gradual descent to the grave. The king of terrors had no power over her. She was to die only to pass out of this world to her Son, only to bless with her hallowed feet the valley of the shadow of death. No coldness, no paleness, no sign of dissolution was to precede her hour of victory. She was to languish of love and die in an ecstacy of its excess. So when the time drew near, she sent for the apostles and gave them her last benediction. She promised to be their mother when she was exalted in heaven. The brightest angels crowded around her, and strains of celestial melody were heard. The watchers who sang " *Gloria in Excelsis*" were there to sing a new song, and heaven came down to welcome the holiest and purest of creatures. Sweetness such as she had never known overwhelmed her. She heard the voice of her child bidding her to come to His arms, and repeating again her *Magnificat:* " My soul doth magnify the Lord, and my spirit hath rejoiced in God my Saviour," she sank away to her eternal rest, and Jesus and Mary were forever united. The humble Virgin had found her hour of victory, and her holy soul was received into the embraces of the Blessed Trinity. As perfection and completeness are the marks of all God's works, so did He finish the work which He had begun. We give Him thanks for His own great glory, and we praise Him for the love He has shown to His mother, for it is His own perfection. The Blessed Virgin lay now like one entranced. The soul had left the body, but corruption could not invade the ark of God, or touch the flesh of which Jesus was born. The odor of heaven filled her humble chamber. The choicest spices of paradise were giving out their fragrance. The apostles knelt, overcome with their nearness to heaven, and filled with the grace which her dying prayer had sent into their hearts. Never could they forget that scene. It nerved them for their baptism of blood. They knew that Jesus was love, but now they had seen with their eyes, and heard with their ears. What a victory was Mary's now! She had lived her appointed time, had lived for God alone. Her labors were all accomplished. She had served her Creator as no creature had served Him before. She had no sorrow and no regret, for she had never for a moment been unfaithful to grace. Now in her perfection and completeness she goes to Him who made her, goes to be queen of all the heavenly host, and mother of all the redeemed. So is she an example for us. We have our labors to discharge in the day of probation. Our appointed time must soon come. We cannot die as Mary did, for we are sinners. Disease and decay must do their work upon us, and our bodily strength must be wasted by anguish and pain. This is the penance we deserve for the sins committed in the body. Corruption will make us its prey, and our sinful dust must return to the dust of which it came. This will be our only way of purification. But the likeness of Mary's death may still be ours, if like her we seek for God alone, and thirst for union with Him. Could we by penance and prayer pay our debt to the divine justice, then the hour of death would be the hour of our triumph. If by constant fidelity to the Holy Spirit we could break the chains which bind to earth, and master the tyranny of self-love, then what power would the adversary have to torment us in that hour? If the soul were really united to God and wholly purified, the last agony would be our entrance upon eternal bliss. And why is not this possible to us? Grace is not wanting, and all we need is a firm resolve and a steady will. Let the death of Mary by its very loveliness attract us to seek to die to all the things of sense, and above all to ourselves. The mystical death must precede the natural death. We must be fast locked in the embrace of Jesus, and then no harm can betide us, for everything must bring us nearer to God. Let not past sin nor present infidelity discourage us. He who died for us loves us wih a love far exceeding our comprehension. He will heal the wounds of the past and help us up the steep ascent. Mary's death will be our encouragement in the last contest; by her example and her prayers we shall be victors over every foe. A good death will be our last and crowning triumph. It will be no trial to us to go where the feet of Jesus and Mary have trod, for there is no darkness where the light of their presence has made the grave the door of entrance to heaven, the gate to a blessed immortality. As Mary is our consoler in every vicissitude of life, so will she be our protector in death.

CHAPTER XX.

THE ASSUMPTION OF THE BLESSED VIRGIN—DAY OF UNION.

"Who is she that cometh forth as the morning rising, fair as the moon, bright as the sun, terrible as an army set in array?" "Who is this that cometh up from the desert, flowing with delights, leaning upon her Beloved?'—CANTICLES, vi. 9; viii. 5.

ALL God's works are complete and perfect. There can be nothing wanting in the harmony of His operations. It was fit that when for love of us He proposed to become incarnate, He should prepare a mother as worthy as possible of Himself. It was fit that that mother should be the purest and most holy of creatures. Anything less than this would shock our ideas of His infinite perfection. So was Mary created a very marvel of purity and grace. And all the providences of God conspired to dignify and sanctify her. God ever treated her as His mother, and will ever treat her as such throughout eternity. It would be impossible for any human creature to honor her as He has honored her. Any other course than this would be unworthy of Him, and a derogation from His divine perfection. We have meditated upon the life and death of Mary. It now remains to see that glory which she had merited, and which her Son was bound to give her, both by justice and by filial love. The holy soul of the Blessed Virgin had found its glorious place in Heaven, but this was not enough for the mother of God. Of her sinless and virginal body the Son of the Highest was born. He was enthroned in the very flesh and blood which He drew from her. It was meet that her body too should put on immortality, and take its share in the mediatorial kingdom. Her own great sanctity merited this of God. Enoch and Elias had been translated in the days before the incarnation. The saints of the old law who had risen with Christ, had followed His triumphal ascent. Why should she, who had been holier than all, be kept in waiting till the day of judgment? If sanctity were any title to this privilege, her claim was beyond that of all others. But she was conceived without sin, and freed by special grace from all the effects of the original curse. Death was one of these effects, with its heritage of shame and corruption. Mary was not under the law of death, and the grave had no claim upon her body. Why then should she be condemned to lie in the earth, and see the ignominy of dissolution? Besides, it could never accord with the great plan of redemption that the Mother of God should know corruption. Decay could not touch the flesh of Jesus, because it was the flesh of God. In like manner the sacred body of which He was made was to be preserved intact. When the Son was ascended on high, the mother yearned for her child, but the child no less yearned for the mother. Mary was no more a mother than Jesus was a son. His human heart yearned continually for the glory of His redeemed, and above all for the honor due to His mother. He could not sit down in the eternal throne in the flesh which He took from her, with her very lineaments and features, and leave her to the shame and penance of corruption. Moreover, the great office which she was to discharge required her complete glorification, her presence in body and soul to intercede for fallen man, and to bring him to a perfect restoration. These motives, which are taught us by the analogies and necessities of faith, are sufficient to warrant us in demanding, in advance of any revelation, the assumption of the Blessed Virgin. . In accordance with all these reasonings the church of God comes in with her constant belief and universal teaching, and bids us give thanks to God, and rejoice because the lowly Virgin has been exalted to the right hand of her Son in Heaven.

When the few days of mourning for the loss of Mary were over, the apostles bore her incorrupt and fragrant body to the valley where Jesus had taught and suffered. There they laid her in a new tomb as they had laid their master. And there they came day by day to watch and pray. It was a quiet spot, which reminded them of their Lord, and which seemed like the antechamber of Heaven. There lay the "pillar of smoke of aromatical spices, of myrrh and frankincense, and of all the powders of the perfumer."* It was she of whom the Beloved said, "My sister, my spouse is a garden enclosed, a fountain sealed up. Thy plants are a paradise of pomegranates with the fruits of the orchard. Cypress with spikenard, spikenard and saffron, sweet cane and cinnamon, with all the trees of Libanus,

---

* Canticles, iii. 6.

myrrh and aloes, with all the chief perfumes."* One day the disciples came to the tomb, and the body of the Virgin was gone. The door was open and the grave-clothes were laid upon the empty stone. Angels were singing their canticles of praise, telling how the Lord came down in power and bore in triumph the most beautiful body of His mother into Heaven. There was a triumphal ascent, as when He first led captivity captive, a gorgeous procession of angels to participate in the joy of the Incarnate God. This was all that man could know. But what must have been the joy of the Blessed Trinity, of the angelic spirits, and of Mary herself. God the Father welcomed His own daughter, in whom He had ever been well pleased. The Son clasped to His bosom His own mother, and she was pillowed once more upon the sacred Heart. "I to my Beloved, and my Beloved to me." The Holy Ghost was the support of His spouse in that consuming glory which no unaided creature can bear

* Canticles, iv. 12-14.

and live. Angels and archangels and seraphs crowded around the throne to bless the great Creator for this most perfect work of His hand. And Mary herself was lost in transports of wonder and love. Now she had found a perfect union with her Son. In soul and body she was His, and never could she be separated from Him. She "found Him whom her soul loved, she held Him and would not let Him go." The glory which belongs to her as the Mother of God it is not for us to imitate, and yet the path which she trod is open to all her children. Unworthy, and sinful as we are, the Son of God redeemed us, and His redemption signifies our complete union with Himself. He could have redeemed us in other ways; He has seen fit to redeem us by taking our nature. So He purposes nothing less for us than the glorification of our souls and bodies in His eternal kingdom. Our bodies shall indeed sleep in the dust and be mingled with the earth; but if they sleep in Him, the day of final resurrection shall call them to His right hand, to the feet of His blessed mother, to the unending joys of Heaven. We shall find perfect union to God, and He alone shall fill every faculty of body and soul. In anticipation of this great consummation let us seek now to draw closer to Him, and learn to turn from everything which would separate us from His love. He is a jealous lover of souls, demanding for his nuptial embrace a heart wholly pure and wholly detached from earthly things. In proportion as we seek Him, shadows shall flee away, darkness shall be driven out of His dwelling place, and He will take us by the hand and gently lead us. Would to God that we were ready for His espousals. But we must first seek purity from every sin, and every affection to sin, and then by a pure intention seek and follow His footsteps. As Mary is our model, so shall she be our guide.

CHAPTER XXI.

THE CORONATION OF THE BLESSED VIRGIN. DAY OF REST.

"Come from Libanus, my spouse, come from Libanus, come; thou shalt be crowned from the top of Amana, from the top of Sinai and Hermon, from the dens of the lions, from the mountains of the leopards." CANTICLES iv., 8.

AFTER the Blessed Virgin had been assumed into heaven, she received the crown which her great offices and her merits had earned. Although God crowns His own gifts in His creatures, nevertheless, He crowns them by a strict justice and by the obligation of His promises. Man cannot think a really good thought without His aid, and yet His greatest gifts never infringe upon our free-will. He promised to reward the cup of cold water given to a disciple in his name. He promised a throne to the apostles, and St. Paul looked forward to the reward. "There is laid up for me a crown of justice, which the Lord, the just judge will render to me at that day; and not to me only, but to all them who love His coming."* As the merits of the Blessed Virgin tower above those of all the saints, so her crown far exceeds in glory. As she has an especial office in the mediatorial kingdom, so her throne is erected at the right hand of her Son. It was not enough then for her to be taken up to heaven. All who enter that celestial palace are kings and priests to God, all wear crowns and bear palm-branches of victory. The Mother of God must receive her crown, and take possession of her seat of honor. So in accordance with catholic tradition, we find her last and highest glory in the ceremony of her solemn coronation. Angels led her to the feet of her Son. He raised her up, and placed her by His side on the shining throne He had prepared for her, and God the Father, Son, and Holy Ghost placed upon her head the bright crown.

* 2 Epistle St. Timothy, iv., 8.

The queen of heaven was enthroned, to the glory of the eternal Trinity and to the joy of patriarchs, and prophets, apostles and confessors, virgins and all· saints. There was nothing more that Mary could ask, for God, infinitely just and true, had more than fulfilled His promises. Here she found rest.—And when we look back through the wonderful life we have so faintly portrayed, when we consider its labors and sorrows, we find every mystery solved and all the divine providences clear. From the immaculate conception to the solemn coronation in heaven, all God's ways are in harmony. The same hand that woke creation out of nothing, and balanced the planets in their courses, formed and fashioned Mary, and led her from Bethlehem to Calvary, and from earth to her eternal rest. There is nothing wanting in this circle of the divine operations, and an overwhelming sense of the perfection of God's works prostrates us in love and wonder at His feet. "O Lord, our Lord, how admirable is Thy name on the whole earth. What is man that Thou art mindful of him, or the son of man that thou visitest him?" Mary had her great and peculiar privilege as the mother of God; but aside from her divine maternity, she is only the model of a just soul. God called her, and she obeyed in every call. She was never unfaithful to His word or His grace. Hence she grew from day to day in knowledge and sanctity, and as the shining light she grew brighter and brighter till her light mingled with the perfect day of heaven. The voice of her Beloved called her from Libanus to be crowned, away from the dens of the lions, and the mountains of the leopards, away from the habitations of the adversary, from the power of every foe. She had ministered to Him; now He will minister to her. She had seen labor and sorrow and martyrdom; now she enters upon an unending rest. In this path the great Sanctifier of souls seeks to lead us. We have our warfare and our hardships, and then our reward. Alas! we are so earthly and indifferent to divine things that we scarcely venture to look forward to joys eternal. Between sanctity and beatitude there is a natural and necessary relation, and conscious of our sinfulness, we dare not anticipate the bliss of heaven. Many only aspire to be just free from sin which kills the soul, and have no longings for holiness. Yet this imperfect state between life and death is not the normal condition of a regenerate soul. We are called to higher things. Our Creator has chosen us for His own. He has breathed into us His spirit. He seeks a perfect union between our hearts and Himself. And when the intellectual man finds earthly things to be vanity, how shall the regenerate man be in peace when he tramples upon any of the instincts of his spiritual life? Is this then the lot of the pilgrim? Must we be ever contending with our enemies, and shall we find no rest this side the grave? Yes! this must be our course until we shall be confirmed in grace. We have the world to subdue in every point, the devil to overcome, and, worse than all, our own self-love to extinguish. There will be no rest until these adversaries are vanquished. And yet if we give up the battle we shall lose all, and even the hope of peace hereafter. Is it too hard for us to follow the steps of Jesus and Mary? Are we not animated by Mary's life and its glorious end? It is at least well for us to look forward to the consummation of our course, and the end of our warfare. There remaineth a rest for the people of God. We may persevere and find that rest, when no temptation can come near us, when even the memory of the past shall torment us no longer. God has a crown in store for us, a mansion prepared, where peace flows as a river and justice as the waves of the sea. The lions shall be chained in their dens, and the leopards confined to their mountains. The hope of this rest should be our consolation in the ever-changing batt'e of life. It is this hope which cheers on the saints in their wonderful labors. The grave loses all its terror. The spiritual world becomes ever near to us, and is more really present to us than the things of sense. And God whom alone we seek, and in whom we live, manifests Himself to us and often grants a foretaste of heaven even while we are in the way. If He is so good to us here, what will He be when we see Him face to face? Mary, seeing God on earth and gloriously crowned in Heaven, is the picture of a just soul led by grace here and rewarded with glory hereafter. Let us ask of God to give us strength to follow her example, and let us begin now by a faithful correspondence with every inspiration of His Holy Spirit. Let our ears be open to hear His voice, and our wills quick to obey. Let our eyes be shut to the world, and open to Him alone, and His unerring providence will lead us safely. He will be our shepherd, and we can alway exclaim with the psalmist, "The Lord ruleth me, and I shall want nothing. He hath set me in a place of pasture. He hath brought me up on the water of refreshments; He hath converted my soul. He hath led me in the paths of justice, for His own name's sake. Though

I should walk in the midst of the shadow of death, I will fear no evils, for Thou art with me. Thy rod and thy staff, they have comforted me. Thou hast prepared a table before me against them that afflict me. Thou hast anointed my head with oil, and my chalice which inebriateth me, how goodly is it? And thy mercy will follow me all the days of my life, that I may dwell in the house of the Lord forever."*

CHAPTER XXII.

THE OFFICE OF THE BLESSED VIRGIN.

"I made that in the heavens there should arise light that never faileth, and as a cloud I covered all the earth. I dwelt in the highest places, and my throne is in a pillar of a cloud." ECCLESIASTICUS, xxiv. 6—7.

THE rapid and imperfect view we have taken of the joys, sorrows and glories of the Blessed Virgin, prepares us for a better

* Psalm, xxii.

appreciation of the great office she discharges in the economy of redemption. Every creature has its place and its proper vocation throughout the whole universe of God. There is nothing without its use and end. The intelligent creatures to whom God has given free will can accept or refuse His gracious purposes, but under all circumstances they must contribute to His glory. If they will not magnify His mercy they must illustrate His justice. The happiness of the creature consists in perfectly corresponding to the end for which he was created. So in the spiritual kingdom which our Lord has set up, apostles, martyrs, confessors, virgins, and even the humblest Christians, have their proper places and their especial offices. The mother of God has an office peculiar to herself, being necessary to the incarnation, a sharer in the mysterious passion of Christ, and a channel of grace to all others. We do not limit in any way God's omnipotence. We do not say that He could not have redeemed the world in any other way than the one He has chosen. But He chose to take our nature into union with His divine nature, and to become flesh. To accomplish this a mother was necesssary, and Mary was therefore a necessity in the plans of God. The redemption purposed could not be effected without her, and she enters into the work of salvation as one of its great actors. She, only a creature, was to have her Creator for her child. This was her office to conceive in her womb, to bring forth, to nourish the eternal Word, and to act towards Him the part of a mother in time and eternity. We say in eternity, because as her relation once existing, must endure forever, so her duties flowing from that relation could never cease. And all Mary's glory flows from the great relation in which she stands to God. No doubt she would have been the greatest of saints if God had not been pleased to make her His mother Yet she owes all her peculiar privileges to the part she had in the incarnation. And in truth she could not be the mother of our Lord without the privileges which faith ascribes to her. It was, therefore, to fit her for her office, that she was conceived without sin, that God continually accumulated upon her the riches of His grace. As a necessary consequence of her dignity, she was assumed into Heaven, and seated upon a throne such as it was fit that the eternal Son should give His mother. And as her infinitely perfect child can never forget His filial duty, so she through all eternity can never forget the offices which flow from her maternal relation. She is more than any other creature interested in the glories of Jesus, and in the extension of His kingdom ; and therefore more than any one but God is she concerned in the sanctification and salvation of souls. And as prayer is the appointed means of obtaining favors from above, so her intercessions must avail more with her Son than the prayers of all other creatures. There is, moreover, an especial power springing from the share which she had in the passion of Christ. She, alone of all, whom He redeemed, suffered with Him, and she found a real martyrdom in His death. Her union with His suffering was indeed a necessity in the divine plans. She could not avoid her great cup of agony, and Jesus could not be baptized with blood without also covering His mother with the crimson flood. In all things her will was free, and she entered voluntarily into the awful tragedy to act her part, forced by no constraint, but giving herself a free-will offering. Since she had such a share in the agonies by which man was redeemed, how can we doubt that she has a peculiar office in the application of the passion? It was promised to the suffering victim that He should see of the travail of His soul, and be satisfied. Why should not the afflicted mother have her great share in this satisfaction? By her martyrdom she not only added to her wonderful merits, but she established a new claim upon the gratitude of her Son. The sorrows which were the life of the world broke her heart, and gave her an especial right to see the fruit of those sorrows, to seek the lost and ruined sinner, and to bind up his hideous wounds. Some of the saints do not hesitate to call her the co-redemptress of the world, not because she was in any proper sense our redeemer, but because of the great office which she has of suffering with Christ, and of applying the saving blood to lost souls. Again, the facts of revelation, as well as the analogies of faith, demonstrate that she is the great channel through which grace flows from God to our fallen race. Jesus loves to convey His gifts through the hands of His mother. He hears her intercessions and grants her the power to dispense His favors. This is the most fitting reward to her merits. When all heaven is interested in the conversion of sinners, she could not sit idle on her throne. When the church of Christ excites the energies of angelic spirits, she cannot rest, who more than all creatures knows the heart of Jesus, and entered into the mysterious depths of the passion. Her prayers bring down daily the dew of heaven upon our barren hearts, and her hands scatter the gifts of His grace wherever there are souls to be roused from death or purified from sin. Every land testifies to her power. Every heart bears witness to her compassion. We feel the perfection and justice of the divine ways, and see how consistent throughout is the plan of salvation. Mary, next to the humanity of our Lord, the most beautiful creation of God, bears witness to the hand that formed her. We see how the eternal Word has taken a mother, not only in the necessities of the incarnation, but also for our sakes. He has given her to us for a mother in this valley of tears. "Woman, behold thy son." "Son, behold thy mother." This knowledge brings us to the shore of that great ocean of the divine love, in which our souls hope to be swallowed up for ever. Only through Mary do we see our God as He has revealed Himself, and come to some faint comprehension of the length and depth, and height of that mercy which planned the incarnation. Perhaps the reflections we have made upon Mary's life may bring us to a practical appreciation of her office towards God and man. If this be the result of our meditations, we shall have accomplished much in the work of our sanctification. We cannot conceive of christianity without Mary, and any gospel without her is not the gospel of Christ. As she had the care of the real body of her Son, so to her are committed the interests of His mystical body. She is a "light that never faileth, and her throne is in a pillar of a cloud." And yet her throne is a throne of mercy to which the sinner may ever come with confidence. She has nothing to do with the justice of God; she is the minister of His mercy. To her, therefore, let us look with hope in all the stages of our pilgrimage, and let us commit the care of our souls to her hands. Let us form our hearts after her model, and seek, by the imitation of her virtues, to become in truth her children. She will teach us how to serve God, and how to love her Son. We can never know the sweetness of Jesus, until we have learned at Mary's feet the mysteries of grace which are hidden in the "Word made flesh."

CHAPTER XXIII.

THE FAITH OF MARY.

"I am come into my garden, O my sister, my spouse; I have gathered my myrrh, with my aromatical spices, I have eaten the honeycomb with my honey, I have drank my wine with my milk; eat, O friends, and drink, and be inebriated, O dearly beloved."—CANTICLES, v. 1.

WE have considered the life of the Blessed Virgin and the successive stages by which she ascended to God. We are now briefly to glance at the virtues which adorned her, and which were the fruits of her great sanctity. She was the garden spoken of in the Canticles, full of the choicest fruits and flowers, exhaling the breath of myrrh and aromatical spices, and overflowing with the richness of the earth. We cannot linger long in this garden, nor can we rightly estimate its luxurious sweetness, but yet the slightest view of its varied fruitfulness will be enough to animate our faith and hope, and to bind us with new love to Him whose hand made this most wonderful masterpiece of His creation. We begin with faith, because by faith man learns to know God, and overcomes the world. "This is the victory which overcomes the world, even our faith." We shall find in Mary all the degrees of a most perfect faith. We see in her whole life a most implicit trust in God, and confidence in His providence. By her immaculate conception she was exempt from the darkness of ignorance, and in all the dealings of God was able to see His hand. Clouds and mystery were about her, and yet she never doubted the divine purposes. Her faith was tried in the circumstances of her early life, when the archangel announced to her her great dignity, when St. Joseph was left to doubt of her purity, and in every step of our Lord's sufferings. Not for one moment did she hesitate or waver in her trust in God, nor did a cloud for one moment cast a shadow over the brightness of her faith. In all things she saw God, and adored His wonderful ways, even when to flesh and sense they were inexplicable. No mortal has ever been compassed about with such strange and marvellous providences, and in all these trials the victory of her faith was perfect. To sustain her in the remarkable lot to which she was called she had a particular trust in God. The divine dealings to her were peculiar, and her faith was peculiar also. She knew from her infancy that her Creator had some great things in store for her, and she threw herself upon Him with the most tender confidence. She had faith in God, and in Him alone, and the tranquility of her spirit could never be disturbed, for He could never break His covenant. This peculiar faith resulted from the reality of her consecration to Him. Nothing was hard or impossible which God purposed; and she had no will but His. Her Maker became her child, and of all His creatures He had none to worship Him with as pure and ardent a faith as hers. She adored Him as her God every moment, and it was her faith which made Him daily more and more dear to her. She saw Him in the manger of Bethlehem, amid the poor and despised of this world, and bending beneath the ignominy of the scourge and the cross. He was not only her own child, He was her God, and this added the overflowing bitterness to her cup of agony. Her faith was so complete that all things earthly were far out of her sight. She lived, and could live for Jesus alone, and everything else was to her as far less than nothing. As the incarnation is the great central mystery of faith, so Mary was the first to understand and adore this mystery. "Blessed is she that believed," when the voice of the archangel first announced this truth. She was the first to adore the Word made flesh when He was conceived in her womb, and every day opened to her new riches in the plan of redemption. She alone teaches us how to understand the incarnation, as she is the the natural protector of the humanity of her Son. All heresies are directed against the truth of our Lord's incarnation, and the love of Mary destroys them all. No false doctrine can abide where she is rightly honored. Nor can any one really believe in the mystery of God manifest in the flesh without appreciating her office. If we could sum up all Mary's faith and love and joy, and express them in one word, perhaps we could hear her say, "Jesus, my God, is my child." "I to my Beloved, and my Beloved to me." In fact, without the incarnation there is no Mary, as without Mary there is no Christ.

And the faith of the Blessed Virgin was active, leading to great works and sustaining her in the unearthly life she had to lead. She believed in the redemption. She felt its power, and knew how the glory of her Son would one day cover the whole earth. She was content to wait God's time, and patiently to do her part. The faithless Jew denied the Redeemer and tracked the precious blood along the streets of Jerusalem. She looked forward to the day when she should apply that blood to heal many a ghastly wound, and to bring peace to many a broken heart. God was alway before her eyes, and in many things her faith was even sight, but great trials perfected her complete confidence in Him. She was so far above the world that the light of heaven ever rested upon her, and yet earth lay beneath her in shadow and cloud. Where she saw not her faith was even better than sight, opening to her a constant and clear view of the invisible.

To imitate our most blessed Mother in this virtue is our only way of salvation, and to closely follow her is a sure path to union with God. We may easily trace all our failures to a want of faith. We wander from the true path, we fall into sin, we are the slaves of pride, and are full of de ects, beca se we do not truly believe what our religion teaches. The things of sense are ever before our eyes, crowding out the view of divine realities, and we make little progress because our aims are low and unworthy of faith. We are all the children of God. Do we truly desire our sanctification, and are we ready for the sacrifices which it involves? Then must we follow Mary in her faith, and look no more upon things seen. We must see the world as God sees it, and count its vanities as less than nothing. We shall learn to hate sin, and to price virtue, and a new earth will open to us with treasures which do not corrupt, and friends which do not deceive. Is not this the elementary idea of the christian life? If we are really members of Christ is not our citizenship in heaven? Is it too much for God to ask us to realize the greatness of His own gifts and the dignity of our vocation? We need faith in the divine providence, faith in God, faith in Christ, faith in the incarnation, and faith in the redemption, and with this faith we can overcome the world, drive it entirely out of our hearts, and put our feet upon its idols. Let us apply this remedy against our besetting sins, and as the attraction of earth diminishes the attraction of heaven will increase. We have not yet looked at our sins in the light of faith, we do not know what miserable creatures we are in

God's sight. Yet His eyes are to be our judge, and we must one day support the scrutiny of His awful justice. Our religion brings us into a spiritual world peopled with angels and saints, where Mary reigns as queen and mother. We are elevated to a life far above the pleasures of worldlings and carnal men. Why should we ever forget what God has done for us, and turn from infinite truth and beauty to the deceiving and unsatisfying joys of sense? One spark of Mary's faith would illumine our whole being, and give a new impulse to all our spiritual energies. We have felt the need of it in our past wanderings from God, we shall feel the need of it still more as trials thicken around us and the shadows of death are thrown across our path. We shall need to grasp the substance of things hoped for, the evidence of things not seen. Mighty miracles of divine love are on every side of us. To see and feel them will be our support in all the perplexities of our pilgrimage.

CHAPTER XXIV.

THE HOPE OF MARY.

"My Beloved is gone down into His garden, to the bed of aromatical spices, to feed in the gardens, and to gather lilies."—CANTICLES, vi. 1.

THE virtue of hope is kindred to faith and springs from it. There can be no hope without faith, and faith can hardly exist in the soul without hope. We should expect to find this virtue in the Blessed Virgin in its utmost perfection, and our expectations cannot be disappointed. In truth her whole life is an exhibition of its power, and she is in all things a model of christian hope. This virtue shone brightly in every stage of her career, and sustained her beneath affliction which otherwise must have crushed her. She ever hoped in God because of His promises, because of His especial love to her, and because of what He had already done for her. Every day, which brought some new manifestation of the divine goodness, added to her hopes. "From henceforth all generations shall call me blessed, for He that is mighty hath done great things to me, and holy is His name." In her joys she looked forward to the accomplishment of God's perfect works. In her sorrows she ever contemplated the end, and not even the darkness of Calvary could take the light from her heart. Her hope was the elastic power which resisted the pressure of woes which no other mere mortal ever endured. She was tranquil under all the adversities of her lot. Her spirit was peaceful as the air of heaven, in the poverty of Bethlehem, in the exile of Egypt, in the cruel tortures of the crucifixion. Her glories were her rewards, and, in the full fruition which they brought her, gave her new reasons to expect great things from her Beloved. When she obtained what she desired, she turned more tenderly towards her child, and hoped more fondly, as her interests and His were blended together. She was never disappointed, but the experience of His perfect fidelity daily raised her to new and heroic heights of hope, until she realized what she longed for, and saw as present what she enjoyed in the future.

We cannot select a single incident of her life where we do not find the power of this virtue. Before the incarnation of our Lord she was constantly looking for the consolation of Israel, and her ardent prayers for the coming of the Messiah were founded upon an unwavering trust in the divine promises. She did not know that she was to be the mother of God. She would not have dared to anticipate such a dignity, yet the union of her heart with heaven taught her that the Orient from on high was soon to visit the world. She was obliged to pass under the shadows which covered the path of her child through this world. She gave Him birth in a stable and took her share in His cup of poverty and human contempt. Hope of better things was the light which made all her darkness sweet.

We see her rising in the night and entering upon a long journey to Egypt, without a murmur or word of discouragement. We see her completely the child of God's providence, taking every dispensation as her own choice, simply because the certain expectation of the reward made everything easy. And her reward was the glory of her child and the extension of His kingdom on earth. We have seen how she supported her loneliness, waiting for the great hour when the interruption of her maternal offices should cease. We have seen her on the way to Mount Calvary, and how she stood patiently beneath the cross She neither fainted nor gave way to human weakness. Brokenhearted, she yet stood strong in hope, with full confidence in God. She went from the sepulchre, repeating the words of the psalmist: "I will bless the Lord, who hath given me understanding. I set the Lord always in my sight; for He is at my right hand that I be not moved. Therefore my heart hath been glad, and my tongue hath rejoiced; moreover my flesh shall also rest in hope. Because thou wilt not leave my soul in hell, nor wilt thou give thy holy one to see corruption. Thou hast made known to me the ways of life, thou shalt fill me with joy with thy countenance; at thy right hand are delights for ever."* The day of the resurrection came to realize her hope, and to reward her faith. And when her Son was taken from her, the thought of her throne so near to His, and of the bright crown His hands were to place upon her head, made cheerful her closing days in this world. Thus hope was one of the bright lilies which bloomed in this garden of the celestial spouse, where the king went to take His repose in the bed of aromatical spices. Hope is a virtue which especially pleases God because it is a constant adoration of His truth and mercy. He has done miracles of love to induce us to trust in Him, and when we throw away all human confidences and look to Him alone, we touch His heart. He will not and cannot disappoint any expectations which are founded

* Psalm, xv. 7-11.

upon His promises. He may try us, and sound the truth of our words, that we may "learn to hold fast the hope set before us, which we have as an anchor of the soul, sure and steadfast." If He bring darkness upon us, it is only to test our sincerity, and to make greater disclosures of His light when every created light shall have been taken away. He wishes us to exhibit the spirit which the Holy Ghost has inspired. "To Thee have I lifted up my eyes, who dwellest in heaven. Behold, as the eyes of servants are on the hands of their masters; as the eyes of the handmaid are on the hands of her mistress, so our eyes are unto the Lord our God, until He have mercy upon us."* Much need have we of this spirit in the trials and discouragements of life. We cannot escape affliction for we are sinners. But the worst of all trials is the experience of our own weakness. We have to learn sooner or later the lesson of our own nothingness. If the dispensations of providence do not teach us this, fearful falls

* Psalm, cxxii. 1–3.

will do it, and if we do not keep up our hope in God, we shall be in danger of despair. When we learn that the creature is nothing, we must at the same time learn that God is everything, or else our experience will not avail to our sanctification. Discouragement is only an evidence of pride and selfishness. We must hope in God always, when frequent falls tempt us to give up altogether our confidence, and when the rod of the divine mercy prostrates us in the dust. Many a soul has realized the words of the psalmist: "My heart hath been inflamed, and my reins have been changed, and I am brought to nothing, and I knew not. I am become as a beast before Thee."* God has a great work to do with our souls. Hope will sustain us while He who knows our frame seeks to purify us. Let us ask Mary to give us her clear view of eternal joys, and let us aspire continually for the things which God has prepared for them who love Him. This will make our pilgrimage cheerful, will comfort us in every trial,

---

* Psalm, lxxii. 21–3.

will give our feet buoyancy in the path of virtue, will gild our dying hour with a light that shall never fade. Hope will be to us the foretaste of the glorious promises which are sealed to us in the blood of the Son of God.

"I am always with Thee. Thou hast held me by my right hand, and by Thy will Thou hast conducted me, and with Thy glory Thou hast received me. For what have I in heaven? and besides Thee, what do I desire upon earth? For Thee my flesh and my heart have fainted away: Thou art the God of my heart and the God that is my portion for ever. It is good for me to adhere to my God, to put my hope in the Lord God. That I may declare all Thy praises in the gates of the daughter of Sion."*

* Psalm, lxxii. 24–8.

CHAPTER XXV.

THE CHARITY OF THE BLESSED VIRGIN.

"I sat down under His shadow, whom I desired; and His fruit was sweet to my palate. He brought me into the cellar of wine, He set in order charity in me."—CANTICLES, ii. 3-4.

As the love of God is the sign of life, so in Mary the spouse of the Holy Ghost we find it in overflowing luxuriance. Her life was a life of love. In fact she lived through love and she died of love. Jesus was impressed "as a seal upon her heart, as a seal upon her arm." Her love was strong as death. Many waters could not quench it, neither could the floods drown it. To love God with the whole heart and soul is the precept of the law, and all Christians are bound to render Him this service. Mary outstripped every command, and went beyond every counsel of perfection. From her first existence she gave her pure heart to God, and she became more entirely His with every breath she drew. Her first reasonable act was an act of love to God, and every act which followed was a new fruit of her love. Every word she spake, every look, every thought, every respiration even was meritorious before heaven, because all she did was animated by her great ruling motive, the divine love. Her whole being was filled with her charity. To God she gave every faculty, every power of soul and body. And all this service was free on her part. No constraint was ever employed to force her obedience. She sought the divine attractions, and as they were daily more and more manifested to her, her will could hardly run fast enough for the impulses of her heart. Her sleep even, as the fathers tell us, was a beautiful offering to her creator. "I sleep," says she, in the Canticles, "but my heart waketh." "In my bed by night I sought Him whom my heart loveth." So perfect a passion for God excluded every affection merely human from her soul. What was all of earth to her? What were its strongest attractions to the eyes which gazed on the infinite beauty? How like an empty bubble appeared to her every created thing, when compared with the immeasurable glories of the Creator? Al. the characteristics of love were found in her in their highest perfection. Hers was a love of attraction since God first drew her to Himself, and her free will obeyed the call. Her love was also a love of gratitude. The favors she had received bound her by a tie of inexpressible sweetness to Him who had so magnified her. She could never do enough to show her thankfulness. He had freed her from every touch of sin, had taken the whole weight of Adam's sin from her shoulders, had lavished upon her the profusion of His grace. He had done more; He had come down from Heaven, and had become her child! He was a true, faithful, loving child to her. Could she ever make return for such favors? All she could do was to throw herself back upon Him with all she had to give—the wealth of that virginal heart which He loved so well. He was everything to her, and she was nothing but what He had been pleased to make her. Her love was also one of preference. She was free to chose the object of her affection, and she chose her God and Him alone. Nothing but God ever moved her will. She had a clear sight of His claims upon her heart, and her whole intellect was filled with His light. She was therefore borne to Him the only choice of her soul, as surely and as steadily as the needle points to the pole. And so she accomplished the love of union which made her one with the object of her love. In this degree of love, the person loving and the object loved meet together by one and a simultaneous action. God, the jealous lover of souls, throws His attractions around the heart, and the heart responds by an instantaneous burst of affection. Or rather the stream of love flows from God, and meets the stream which He sets in motion from the creature, and the two streams are mingled together. The Creator loving extends His arms to embrace the creature, and the creature loving casts itself into that blissful and unending embrace. In such a love everything earthly has vanished out of sight. There is perfect purification from every sin and every affection to sin, and the whole being is illumined with light that pervades every part, and puts every shadow of sense to flight. In Mary there was no need of purification. She was ever purer than the crystal dew of heaven. And from her very conception she was the temple of the Holy Ghost, the tower of David, the tower of ivory and the house of gold. There was no rebellion in her flesh, and no obstacle in her soul to the perfect effect of the divine graces. What she received she gave back to the giver, and in every oblation gave herself. The hearts of Jesus and Mary were the hearts of mother and child, and while one was the heart of God, filled with all His infinite riches, the other was the heart of the holiest of creatures, consuming and overflowing with love. Angel and archangel were mute before the throne of the infinite majesty. Cherubim and seraphim were the very intelligent expression of love, and yet no creature ever loved God as Mary loved Him, as she loves Him now, and as she will love Him through eternity. If we are in any sense the children of Mary, her heart is the model after which we are seeking to form our own hearts. If we have none of her love to God, we are in no sense her servants. The very first thing which she does for the sinner, is to give him a love for her Son. If she cannot accomplish this in us, she can do nothing. Love is the sign of life. It is shed abroad in our hearts by the Holy Ghost, whose indwelling makes us sons of God and heirs of Heaven. Without it we are dead and barren branches of the vine. And even if we find in ourselves some degree of love, by comparing our hearts with Mary's, we shall see how utterly deficient we are in this most necessary of all virtues. The world has such a strong hold upon us that the divine attractions are hardly felt. We mean to serve God, but our purposes, aims and wishes are formed after human models, and breathe a worldly spirit. Few are the generous hearts that freely and unreservedly follow the impulses of grace, to the utter disregard of human respect and human opinion. The flesh is rebellious, a d things sensual have not lost their power over us. We feel the divine attraction, but we respond feebly to it, as if afraid of the sacrifices which may be the consequence. We say we have chosen God for our portion, but our actions belie our words. There is something else which we seek for, some other object of affection, some shapeless hope perhaps which we run after, as it ever eludes our grasp. And the worst of all is, that generally there is some dark corner in our hearts, some wound into which we like not to put the probing knife of the physician. One would think that gratitude would rise above all these obstacles, but alas! gratitude is rarer than love. Here we see the great want of our souls. Here we behold the cause of our imperfection.

We see why we do not daily overcome our defects, why we remain ever as beginners in the way of life. The garden of the Lord is filled with weeds and briars, instead of fruits and flowers. Our resolutions come to nothing, our good intentions die before they result in actions, because the vital flame of love burns so low and feebly in us. We are just alive, and that is all that can be said of the most of us. To be conscious of our need is the first step to restoration, and hence if the picture of Mary's loving heart makes us sensible of our coldness, we shall have accomplished much towards our recovery. Let us pray to her to give us of her own spirit. Let us really turn from earthly things, as she did. God will manifest Himself to us as soon as we make ready to receive His attractions. His love will be the sovereign remedy for all our ills. It will undo the effects of past sin, dispel the power of present temptation, and give peace to the most distracted heart. It will bind up every bleeding wound, and make the wilderness a garden and the desert a paradise.

CHAPTER XXVI.

THE HUMILITY OF THE BLESSED VIRGIN.

"I am the flower of the field, and the lily of the valleys."—CANTICLES, ii., 1.

HUMILITY is the foundation of all virtues, and without it no one can please God. Pride destroys every merit and puts an end to all growth in holiness. The moment the creature exalts himself through consciousness of the divine gifts, he places himself in an attitude of rebellion. As the Blessed Virgin was the holiest of all creatures, so she was of necessity the most humble. In her, self-love was entirely extinct, and God was the only object of every action. As the incarnation was the great act of the divine condescension, so the mother partook of the humility of her child. The same mind was in her that was in her Son.

He was meek and lowly of heart, she was the white lily of the valley, the companion of the humility in which He was pleased to dwell. With all her gifts Mary had always a lowly opinion of herself. She was not unconscious of what God had done for her, but she recognized that the favors she had received were all for the glory of the giver. She was only the handmaid of the Lord, and every new gift He gave her, only increased her debt. It did not stimulate any self-complacency. Rather she was the more abased at the sight of her own littleness, and she thought herself unworthy of any favor. Enveloped as she was with the wonderful displays of divine power, in all she saw only the love and mercy of her Creator. "He hath regarded the humility of His handmaid." "He that is mighty hath done great things to me, and holy is His name." "He hath put down the mighty from their seats, and hath exalted the humble." She was too lowly in spirit to think she was to become the mother of God, although she might have learned it from the wonderful providences which surrounded her. The message of the archangel startled her because she was too humble to dream of such a dignity, and she trembled when Gabriel bent the knee before her, and called her "full of grace." And when Jesus lay in her arms, and she clasped her God to her bosom, her joy left the creature far out of sight to rest alone in the beauty of the creator manifest in the flesh. But though she was conscious of her gifts, she was not conscious of her merits. She set no value on what she did, and she ascribed all her graces to the undeserved love of God, rather than to her own good works. She never thought that her virtues had drawn the eternal Word to her, or that her great reward in heaven was to be the recompense of her fidelity. And she was ever disposed to conceal from others the great favors God had bestowed upon her. When St. Elizabeth called her blessed above all women, and by the impulse of the Holy Ghost gave her praise for the faith she had shown, she simply replied, "My soul doth magnify the Lord." When St. Joseph was permitted to doubt of her integrity, she had no words of defense for herself, but left it for God to teach him the mystery of the incarnation. She never prided herself on her dignity, or before others exacted any of her maternal privileges. She loved the obscurity of her home in Nazareth, where the world knew nothing of her joys, and where St. Joseph and her Son were accounted as laborers. She went to the temple as the law commanded, and made an offering for her purification, when she had never known sin. She appeared before the altar as any ordinary woman, leaving it for God to make known her dignity, if He should see fit, or to leave the world in ignorance of her privileges. And although she was the mother of the Highest, excelling in rank the most glorious archangel, yet the lowliest duties were her delight. She went a long journey to serve her cousin Elizabeth, and remained with her three months. Nothing pleased her more than to minister to others. She became the mother of the disciples of our Lord, and after His resurrection remained on earth to direct and assist the apostles in the foundation of the Church. No one ever came near her, that she did not seek to do them some kindness. It is so now, when she is in heaven, and it will be so throughout eternity. The love of contempt was also a crowning feature in her humility. The poverty of Bethlehem was dear to her. It shut her in a cave, with her child, away from the world. When men despised Him, it wounded her in her tenderest point, but for herself she had no care. In the day of triumph she was not seen. She was not present when the multitude came to take Him by force and make Him a king. When He rode into Jerusalem with the palm-branches waving before Him, and the shout of hosannas rending the air, the mother did not mingle in the general joy. But when the mob were dragging Him in His own blood through the streets, she went out to partake of His cup of ignominy. She stood to the last by the cross, heedless alike of the scorn of her own nation, or the rough jeer of the infidel. In sorrow, contempt, poverty, she was ever at His side, because she loved to be nothing among mankind, since God was everything to her, and the creature nothing. And her course of self-abnegation still continues. She has never vindicated her own honors, except when they concerned the honor of her Son. She has been established in Sion, and has taken root in God's holy mountain, and her throne is in the full assembly of saints. Yet she has never asked for any privilege, but to defend with her own person the rights of her child. She was all for Jesus, without a thought of herself. Such a wonderful degree of humility became the mother of God, and we her children praise the divine wisdom which has given us such a model. Pride is the root of all our evils, and the cause of our many imperfections. We are not only conscious of our gifts, but we even imagine favors which do not belong to us. Scarcely ever do we have a true idea of ourselves. When we sin or wound our Lord by infidelity, we have a ready excuse. When we do any good work, we are quick enough to ascribe it to our own virtues. We fear much that others will take too low an estimate of our merits, and are quite often anxious to make known every advance we make in the way of self-mastery. We cannot easily condescend to do kind offices for others, except when some praise will be our reward. And as for the love of contempt, it is far above ordinary Christians, and has the appearance of fanaticism in those who profess it. It is easy to see that self lies at the bottom of many of our best and holiest actions. Yet with the sincere confession of our weakness, let us not be discouraged. God became incarnate to cure our pride. Mary was the most humble of creatures to be our model. Let us follow in her footsteps. We have had experience enough to convince us that in our own strength we can do nothing. Let us never think of any strength but God's. His arm will be under us if we look to Him alone. And if we really desire conformity with Christ, the heavenly physician will know how to minister to our maladies. He will lead us by paths we could not have conjectured to the valley of self-abnegation, and there teach us to cast off our whole load of sin. Humility then will not be unreal in us, nor hypocritical. It will spring from the thorough conviction of the all-sufficiency of God, and the utter nothingness of all created things. Happy are they who learn this lesson. "Blessed are the poor in spirit, for theirs is the kingdom of God." "He that humbleth himself shall be exalted," and "if we suffer with Christ, we shall also reign with Him."

CHAPTER XXVII.

THE PURITY OF THE BLESSED VIRGIN.

"Thy name is as oil poured out, therefore young maidens have loved thee. Draw me, we will run after thee, to the odor of thy ointments."—CANTICLES, i., 2–3.

No mortal tongue can worthily speak of the purity of the holy mother of God, and yet while we linger in this "house of gold," it is meet to consider a virtue of which she is the great model and exemplification. In body and soul she was wholly consecrated to God, and the infection of sin never came near her. Conceived without sin, she was freed from the effects of the fall and its ignominy. She never knew the stimulus of concupiscence, and there was no rebellion of the flesh against the spirit. The prince of the world came to her, and found nothing in her to correspond with his temptations. Hence he was baffled at every point, and could only address her with external solicitations which were resisted as soon as presented. The degree of holiness to which the Blessed Virgin attained, led her to the most perfect love of God. This love produced a true and real espousal to her celestial bridegroom, and the vow of virginity was the necessary consequence. That vow is only the consecration which love in its highest degree includes. Of all the daughters of Eve, Mary was the first to solemnly devote herself in body and soul to the worship of God. She began that life on earth, which is the angelic life in heaven. And after her many have followed, according to the words of Scripture, "after her shall virgins be brought to the king." Her name hath touched many souls, inspiring them with the divine love, and coming as oil poured out to soothe and heal the wounds of earth. "Therefore young maidens have loved her," and following her attractions, have run after her to the odor of her ointments.

She made her vow in her early years, and she would not have sacrificed her virginity even to be mother of God. She was espoused to St. Joseph with the express understanding that she should ever remain a virgin, and because wonderful designs of providence so ordered. When the archangel Gabriel announced to her that she was to bring forth the Messiah, she did not consent until she was clearly assured that her purity should be preserved intact. It was only when she heard that she was to conceive by the power of the Holy Ghost, that she exclaimed, "Behold the handmaid of the Lord, be it done unto me according to thy word." Thrice precious among all the jewels of heaven is this grace of virginity of which Mary was the example. Her holy soul was also beyond the reach of any contamination. No darkness or ignorance ever clouded its clear view of God and things eternal. Every thought was the inspiration of the Divine Spirit who dwelt in her, and the pure intention with which every act was performed made her least work an acceptable offering in the sight of heaven. In her heart was no place for any merely human affection. If she loved any human thing, it was by love which first went up to God, and then descended from Him to His creatures. In her there was no division of services, no half-way consecration. All was for God. She was a temple filled with His life and light, and ever resounding with His praise. Such purity the creation had not before seen. It was a wonderful condescension to our fallen humanity, that she was made a creature like unto us, instead of a bright angel formed to tread the golden streets of the celestial city, and walk in the midst of the stones of fire. Yet Mary, the second Eve, the mother of the living race, was only a daughter of Adam adopted by God as His own daughter, the mother of His Son, and the spouse of His eternal Spirit.

Of all virtues, perhaps chastity is the most difficult to practise. In our fallen state the flesh ever rebels against the spirit, and the motions of concupiscence are sometimes a heavy trial to the regenerate soul. Sense allures with the sight of apparent good, and our appetites are seduced by the desire of gratification. Without grace we cannot overcome the power of sin in our members. But thanks be to God, who hath given us the victory through Jesus Christ our Lord. Under the new law where sin abounded, grace much more abounds. The Redeemer has wrought a perfect work. He has left grace to counteract every effect of the fall, and His blood has power to cleanse every stain and defilement. He pours His Spirit into our hearts and washes us clean from every transgression. He gives us His own flesh, which is the food of angels, and His own blood, which is the wine that germinates virgins. He gives us the immaculate Mary for our mother, and he brings the young heart to her and seeks to preserve it from the contaminations of the world. What more could infinite love devise? God calls us all to preserve purity according to our state of life. Virginal chastity is not the lot of all His servants. But all are bound to seek Him alone with upright souls, and to be pure in heart. "Blessed are the pure in heart, for they shall see God," shall draw nigh to Him in this life, and experience even on earth His gracious manifestations. And in proportion as we purify our hearts, does the great King come near us, to draw us more completely within the circle of His attractions, and to bring us to oneness with Himself. For all our past sins against this great virtue there is a remedy at hand. A stream purer far than Jordan rolls at our feet. We must wash in it seven times and we shall be clean, and the flesh of a child shall come back to us. For every present temptation we have a ready assistance. Jesus and Mary are ours. We have but to ask, and the arm that prostrated the tempter in the wilderness will hold us up. We have but to call upon Mary, and the serpent whose head she crushed will flee away. The cool breath of the rose of Sharon will revive our fainting spirit; the fragrance of the lily of the valley will throw around us the air of heaven. And for the future let us prize our purity even above all virtues. Let us guard our senses, for the least touch will defile us. One unguarded moment will undo the work of many years. Let us remember that we belong to God, that Jesus is our Master, that Mary is our mother. Whatever grace God may deny us, let us ask Him to give us this most precious jewel of chastity. Let Him bring us into the waters of affliction, or prostrate our strength beneath the wasting power of disease, rather than let us fall victims to sin which defiles the body and kills the soul. And happy are they who can follow closely in Mary's footsteps. The heavenly Bridegroom will be faithful to them. He will lead them into green pastures, and one day they shall follow Him wheresoever He goeth.

CHAPTER XXVIII.

THE POVERTY OF THE BLESSED VIRGIN.

"I have put off my garment, how shall I put it on? I have washed my feet, how shall I defile them?"—CANT. v. 3.

Our blessed Lord Jesus Christ has given us a perfect example of poverty and contempt of the world. Having condescended to take our nature, He chose to be in a lowly and humble position. For our sakes He chose to be "made poor, that we through His poverty might be made rich." He could have enjoyed all the wealth of the world, and all its luxuriance might have rolled at his feet. He could have been born in a palace with thousands to wait upon His every want. But the gifts of earth did not become the humility of the incarnate God. He saw the emptiness of human things, and He would not touch any of the gilded vanities which so attract mankind. It was His will to be driven out of the habitations of men, and to have no place where to lay His head. He preferred a cave for His birth-place, and the oxen's stall for His cradle. His holy mother, whose heart was one with His, took part in His self-abnegation. The world was nothing to her, and all its riches could not excite one emotion in her soul. She gave all she had to the poor, that for the service of God she might be emancipated from every care. The fathers tell us that in her early childhood she made a vow never to possess any of the goods of this earth. "Where our treasure is there also is our heart." She desired to have no treasure here, that her heart might be wholly united to God. It was, therefore, no trial to her to bear the pains and inconveniences of poverty. The cave of Bethlehem was a sweet hiding-place where she could prove to her child that she loved nothing but Him. The Magi brought their costly gifts, and they were devoted to charity. She went before the altar with two turtle-doves, the offering of the poor, and knelt among the crowd. The angel called her at midnight to arise in haste and fly to Egypt. She arose at once, leaving all she had, and began her long and painful journey. Many a time she felt the pangs of hunger and thirst in her pilgrimage through the desert, and during her lonely sojourn in the land of idolatry. Her food was always coarse, and her raiment plain. When the holy family returned to Nazareth, a lowly cottage became their abode, where Jesus, Mary and Joseph all worked with their hands to earn their daily bread. There was no rest for them in this world of sin. The second Adam came to the thorny ground of the first Adam, and took His portion of toil. It was Mary's delight to be among the poor, and even to do menial offices for others. She drank in more and more every day of the spirit of her child, and became more and more detached from every earthly thing. When He left her to begin His ministry she was dependent upon the charity of others.

He was on the mountain, and in the desert, and why should not His mother be a pilgrim like Him? And when He died He gave her in trust to St. John, that the disciple whom He loved might provide for her wants. In Mary's poverty we see not only the entire renunciation of all worldly goods, but a complete separation from them in heart. She had nothing, and she desired nothing. Her soul was most tranquil, because no created thing had power to touch her heart. She had put off all the garments of earth, how could she ever put them on again? She had washed her feet from every defilement of corruptible treasure, how could she touch again the dust of this world? She had only one posession, an infinite one, her God; and this filled her whole heart.

There is much for us to learn in this brief view of the poverty of the Blessed Virgin. The Church commends this virtue as most necessary for all who would tread in the steps of her Master. Actual poverty is no doubt a grace for such as use it rightly. The poor are freed from many temptations, and are not so likely to fasten their affections upon worldly things. Their hard life here is an incentive to look above for enduring treasures. To a certain extent they must feel themselves strangers and pilgrims on their way to a better country. Hence the poor are generally the favored children of God. The Lord was surrounded by them when He was on earth, and His church is espe ially their portion. But poverty of spirit is essential for all who would be saved. We must learn to despise worldly things, or we can make no real progress in the love of God. Whatever goods of earth God may give us, we must not fix our affections upon them, nor desire them for their own sake. As good christians we must be detached from the treasures of which we are only stewards. Our Lord Himself has said that it is hard for the rich to enter into His kingdom, and that they who trust in riches have no hope of salvation. With the possession of wealth comes care, which weighs upon the soul, and bears it down among the pursuits of time. Many spend their whole lives in toil and labor, and have no reward but treasures which one hour may take away, and which can never go beyond the grave. The brief joys of the rich will never pay for the anxious mind or the aching heart. If we are poor we must bless God for this grace, and endeavor to turn it to our sanctification. If we are encumbered with the possessions of this life, we must use them for the benefit of our neighbors, as well as our own salvation. We must make to ourselves friends of the mammon of iniquity, that when we fail they may receive us into eternal habitations. The Catholic religion, animated by the spirit of its divine Head, has taught us many heroic lessons in the virtue of poverty. It has taught many souls to emulate the graces of Mary, and cheerfully to lay down at the feet of Jesus every temporal thing. Princes have descended from their thrones to cast the dust of this world from their feet, and to be wholly emancipated for the service of God. The vow of poverty is a necessary condition of the religious state, since perfect consecration of the soul is inconsistent with any hold upon the things of this life. No one can leave the world except by renouncing all that he has, and by choosing alone a heavenly treasure. "If thou wilt be perfect, go and sell what thou hast and give to the poor, and follow me, and thou shalt have treasure in heaven."

The example of the Blessed Virgin will be our encouragement, as we endeavor to walk in her footsteps. She will gently wean us from the love of all earthly possessions, guiding us, as we can bear it, to a more and more perfect life. We need not be discouraged at the sight of our own self-love, nor at our great repugnance to mortification. We shall not learn detachment all at once, nor in the easy way our imaginations have pictured. But with Mary for our model we cannot wander from the right path. As things temporal recede little by little from our view, things eternal will draw nearer to us. The chains that bind us to earth will be broken one by one, and the love of God will be the only solace of our free spirits. Who would compare corruptible treasures with the infinite wealth of God, who becomes Himself the possession of His saints?

CHAPTER XXIX.

THE OBEDIENCE OF THE BLESSED VIRGIN.

" To my company of horsemen in Pharao's chariots have I likened thee, O my love. Thy cheeks are beautiful as the turtle dove's, thy neck as jewels. We will make thee chains of gold, inlaid with silver."—CANTICLES, i. 8–10.

By disobedience our first mother Eve lost Paradise, and left to us an inheritance of shame. The second Eve, who was to restore us to our birthright, accomplished her task by a life of perfect obedience. The service of God requires the submission of all our faculties to His will. The laws which He gives us are only the expression of the eternal and unchangeable counsels of the divine Being. A creature endowed with free will can resist the purposes of the Creator, but by so doing he frustrates the end for which he was made. An intelligent obedience is not only the tribute due to the Author of our existence, it is also the only way of happiness. Pride excites us to rebel against the divine counsels, and has been the cause of our ruin. The Blessed Virgin began the work of our reparation by a just and true service of God. In every act of her whole life she was guided by the sincere desire to obey the voice of the Holy Spirit, and hence she never sought for one instant her own pleasure. All that self would dictate she utterly renounced, and every moment her whole being was a sacrifice to God. Her soul desired nothing but Him, her heart loved nothing but Him, and her intellect knew nothing but Him. Being exempt by her especial privilege from original sin, the disorders of the fall never reached her. There was never rebellion in any part of her being, nor even an impulse contrary to the wishes of her Beloved. He had but to speak and instantly she obeyed, and His work and her co-operation kept pace in her soul. So is she compared to a company of horsemen hastening after the voice of their captain ; and the chains of gold inlaid with silver are the symbol of the perfect union of will between herself and her celestial spouse. Since then every breath she drew was an act of obedience, it is hard to particularize the proofs of her heroic conformity to the divine pleasure. In her early life she offered herself to God, because His voice called her to the sacrifice, and the irrevocable vow was only the expression of her self-abnegation. The office of Mother of God was freely accepted by her, with a full knowledge of the pains it involved. The spirit of her life was according to her words, "Behold the handmaiden of the Lord ; be it unto me according to thy will." She took a long journey to Bethlehem, led by the Holy Spirit, that according to prophecy she might bring forth the Son of God in the city of David. Blind obedience led her to the stable, to the despised village of Nazareth, to the lonely sojourn in Egypt. It was her consolation never to have any desire of her own, and hence every event of providence found her prepared. We have seen the Son of the highest bowed down to the earth in Gethsemane, while blood gushed from every pore of His body. We have seen the God-man lifted upon a cross between two thieves, drinking to the dregs the cup of the world's scorn and contempt. A spectacle like this man had never seen before, and shall never see again. But next to this astounding picture, is the sight of the broken-hearted mother, standing beneath the accursed tree and offering up her infinite treasure, her only child, all she had. No mere creature ever approached this act of self-renunciation. As obedience raised the knife by which our father Abraham prepared to slay his only son, so obedience sublime and wonderful fastened the afflicted Virgin to the foot of the cross. In all she adored the divine purposes, in darkness as in light, in the shadows of death as in the splendors of the resurrection. Obedience had reached its height. Calvary was its test. Mary gave God back to God, and not in the tender beauty of infancy as she received Him, but with bruised and mangled limbs crimsoned with His own blood. The sinner may draw near the cross which he prepared for Mary's Son, and learn the lesson of submission to God's will. If he cannot learn it here, there is no teacher who can instruct him. Our lives have been made up of rebellions, and our free wills have often been employed to dishonor our creator and to contemn His laws. We could have given Him much glory before men and angels, and we have refused to pay Him our tribute. Disobedience to His voice is the cause of every misery we have experienced, and there is but one remedy for our manifold infirmities. We must trample under foot our own will, and by fidelity to all divine inspirations seek to recover the graces we have lost. Regeneration made us in truth the children of God with the docility which belongs to the heart of a child. "We must humble ourselves and become as little children" if we desire to enter into the kingdom of Heaven. All God's providences are directed for our sanctification. Not a sparrow falls to the ground without His knowledge, and even the hairs of our heads are numbered. Is it not easy to throw ourselves into the arms of His fatherly care, and to be led by His all-perfect counsels? In the spiritual life He calls us to many trials. No character could be perfected without painful lessons of the nothingness of human promises. Yet wherever there is the earnest purpose to obey, there is alway light enough to illumine our footsteps. We need not to behold the distant scene when present duty is clear, and the voice of conscience gives us its plain admonition. God calls the sinner to repent of his sins, and to cut himself off from all dangerous occasions. He calls a thousand times, and often His call is totally disregarded. He seeks continually the perfection of the just, and bids them aim for higher and higher degrees of holiness. We hear His voice, but we have not the inclination or the courage to obey Him. So He can do very little with our souls, and there is no chance for us but in the scourges of His anger, or in the purifying flames of justice. How much better would it be for us to yield Him a loving heart and to let His great mercy accomplish its work in us. "Blessed are the undefiled in the way, who walk in the law of the Lord."

That we may not lose the fruit of these reflections, let us directly apply them to our own hearts, and ask our consciences to tell us the duty which at this moment God requires of us. The answer will often come before we ask the question, and then if we desire any part in Mary's reward, we must imitate her obedience. At once, and with zeal we must do the work which our heavenly Master commands, and we shall find our labors light and our toil even refreshing. From the way of life our feet shall never wander, for He who is our guide can never err. Step by step we shall leave the valley behind us, and ascend the mountain where God gathers His elect, and where the human will lays itself down at the feet of the divine perfections. If we hesitate and seek to serve the world as well as God, we shall either fall altogether from the state of grace, or lead a cold and unhappy life, constantly tasting of remorse, and treasuring up fearful regrets for the hour of death. Who can estimate the results of one false step, or tell the evils that shall flow from one disobedience? Many a soul which would have glorified its creator through the long ages of eternity, is now agonizing in the eternal fire because of one transgression. There are souls just hanging between life and death, and the next act shall decide their destiny. And many of us for whom perhaps God designed high perfection, have wandered from the narrow path, when the heavenly goal was almost in view; and one slight infidelity was the turning point in our probation. Happy indeed was Mary to have been the mother of her God, but happier far that always and in every thing she heard His word and kept it.

CHAPTER XXX.

THE PATIENCE OF THE BLESSED VIRGIN.

"The keepers that go about the city found me; they struck me and wounded me. The keepers of the walls took away my veil from me."—CANTICLES, v. 7.

As humility is the foundation of virtue. so patience is the beautiful crown of a just soul, giving gracefulness and honor to all its works for God. There are two kinds of patience, one which consists in waiting upon the divine will, and another which leads to the improvement of suffering. The first is in reality a trial of our obedience, since as God is our creator He has a sovereign right to dispose of us and of all human things according to His own pleasure. Man is naturally selfish and unwilling to leave all his desires in the hands of Providence. Our purposes often ripen faster than the designs of God, and it is hard to rest quietly without any care for the results of our labors. Yet we can never wholly please Him, unless we are content to act with that end alone in view. If we seek for an immediate reward, or are anxious to see the fruits of our labors, we shall make little progress in the way of holiness. Even in the affairs of this world we can never be truly successful without patience, but in the spiritual life we can accomplish absolutely nothing. For new difficulties present themselves at every step, as temptations multiply and the great weakness of our own hearts manifests itself. As the husbandman toils carefully in the spring and then awaits the harvest, so we must labor in hope and faith, leaving it for God to give the increase in His own time. But suffering is also a law of progress in the regenerate soul, and we can get back to the paradise we have lost only by pain. There is sorrow of heart and agony of body, and both are necessary to our purification. "He that hath suffered in the flesh, hath ceased from sins." The road of the cross is the royal road of sanctification. Great patience is required to bear well the afflictions of our probation, and to turn them to the profit of our souls. The Blessed Virgin is a perfect model of this virtue in all its degrees, and under all its trials. No creature was ever the subject of such peculiar and strange providences. She was in the hands of God without a care for herself, and as His purposes developed, she was more and more anxious to renounce her own desires. She left Him to fulfil His promises in His own time, certain that He would never fail her, and filled with increasing admiration at His wonderful ways. She was in the midst of mysteries half-opened, where the divine hand was surely operating, but where flesh and sense were forced to be tranquil. Now her celestial spouse appeared to her full of grace, and oil was upon His lips. Now He came up from the desert stained with blood, and clouds and darkness were round about Him. In every shape she recognized Him, and meekly awaited His will. Never for one instant did she have recourse to any human means, or seek to accomplish anything by plans of her own devising. She labored in His garden and at His word, and she had nothing to do when He held her hands. If He gave no success to her toil, it gave her no pain, for she sought not success, but only His favor. Hence she was never in haste, nor for a passing moment lost her tranquillity. Quiet, calm and peaceful was the work going on in her soul, and yet her progress was more rapid than the flight of the eagle as he leaves far behind the high mountains of earth. So has He promised, " They that hope in the Lord shall renew their strength, they shall take wings as eagles, they shall run and not be weary, they shall walk and not faint." In our brief view of Mary's dolors we have seen how she drank the cup of sorrow, and was baptized in the blood of her Son. The shadow of the cross was over her whole life, enveloping in its darkness even her brightest hours. And all her pains were unmerited, and came to her as the precious gift of her child, and the fruit of her union with Him. Her different griefs pierced every portion of her maternal heart, and the sword of Simeon was never withdrawn from her bosom. Patience, sublime and wonderful, sustained her in agonies, which without special grace would have extinguished her life. In the night of her third sorrow she walked alone in the waste of human woe, without even the rod and staff of her Son. Disease could not touch her fair form, because the immaculate flesh of the mother of God was beyond the reach of decay. But the anguish of her soul in the sufferings of Jesus made her frame to tremble, and drank up the fountains of her innocent life. Follow her on the journey to Calvary, where the rude rabble made her a mark for their insults. Behold her embracing the cross in the darkness which had terrified even the inhuman murderers, and waiting six long hours that the cup of sorrow might be drained to its dregs, that God's love might be satisfied, and man's malignity satiated. See her calmly walking to the sepulchre to lay the beloved of her heart upon His stony bed, and then patiently going to the house of St. John to await the resurrection. And when He ascended to His Father, she was left alone once more, to bear her exile until the days of her great sanctity were accomplished, and the chariot of fire should bring her to His everlasting embrace. Perfected by patience, and full of merits by suffering, she passed to the throne of her own child. She is an example of that entire submission to God which is the end of the Christian life. As the angels quietly, peacefully and yet swiftly do His will in Heaven, so did she on earth obey the divine voice, running faster than thought after its every whisper, and yet never anxious, never weary, but tranquil as the infant Jesus when first He lay upon her breast.

We must imitate her in this patience, if we desire to attain conformity with God. The work of our sanctification shall go on, but not as we have imagined, and our road to heaven shall not be the one which our fancies have pictured. That path lies through valleys, around the base of high mountains, and up the steep ascent of cragged hills. Many of our plans shall be frustrated, and our dearest hopes often disappointed. We shall toil long and see no fruit of our labors. The bright blossom of spring shall fall to the ground, and wither in the heat of the sun. Let man be silent when God works, and when the great husbandman walks in His garden, let the creature be patient. And when the cross brings its sacred weight to our shoulders, let us improve the day of grace. We suffer because we are sinners, and because past transgression has left its mark upon our souls. That mark must be burnt out by salutary pain, until every trace of defilement vanishes before the refiner's fire. The penitent need not fear in the hour of God's greatest mercy The sinner who goes to Calvary bears in his flesh the proofs of the divine favor. What though disease should prey upon our bodies, and like a worm eat away the vigor of our physical life? The chastened flesh will be a more fitting habitation for the purified soul, and the veil of sense will melt before our eyes. Pride will be laid low before the altar, and self-love will be the victim of the sacrifice.

CHAPTER XXXI.

THE PRAYER OF THE BLESSED VIRGIN.

"Thy lips, my spouse, are as a dropping honeycomb, honey and milk are under thy tongue; and the smell of thy garments as the smell of frankincense."—CANTICLES, iv. 11.

PRAYER is the simple act by which the creature realizes his dependence upon the Creator, and supplicates His favor. It is the appointed way of obtaining graces, since God, however disposed to shower His benefits upon us, requires some disposition on the part of the receiver. There is, then, no spiritual life without prayer, and he who neglects this mean of salvation can have no hope of divine mercy. The very first impulse of the Holy Ghost is to turn the heart to Him from whom all life proceeds, and every breath of the good christian ought to be a supplication for that assistance, without which there is no good word or work.

We are in the daily need of temporal blessings, and can accomplish absolutely nothing in the supernatural order without spiritual aid. The sense of our own weakness naturally turns the soul to the infinite fountain of all life and strength, and hence the more we understand our own necessity the better we are able to pray. For prayer no art is required. Any expression of our wants to God is acceptable prayer, whether the tongue reverently speaks to Him, or the eyes look to Him, or any of our senses signify the desire of the heart. Vocal prayer is the lowest degree, and from this we ascend to meditation, to contemplation, and even to union with the maker of our spirits. In meditation the soul separates tself from all sensible things to apply itself to eternal truths, and to discover the divine will. God's revelation is thus brought home to the individual, and the unchanging verities of faith are made real and practical to our minds. Contemplation carries us a step higher, lifting the understanding to a certain fruition of the object and author of truth, and fastening all the powers of the soul in a firm gaze upon Him, who always reveals Himself in every light He gives. And they who really aim after perfection may attain to that prayer of union of which the saints have written, and which no human language can describe. It is the mutual embrace of God and the soul that seeks Him, where the creature who receives everything, finds himself in the arms of Him whose bounty gives everything, and even gives Himself. There is no limit to the desire of the sanctified soul, even as there is no end to the prodigality with which God lavishes his favors. In the blessed mother of our Lord we find an example of the highest degree of prayer, and an instructor in this most important lesson of the spiritual life. Her communion with her Maker began before her birth, when the strong hand of her Redeemer drove the adversary away, and chased every shadow of the fall from her understanding. Then ascended to heaven the acceptable incense of her pure spirit, passing beyond the golden censors of the angels to the immediate presence of her Beloved. The stages of perfection were passed, and when she opened her eyes upon this world of sin, she was bound to God by a union which no power could disturb. The all-merciful Creator took the soul of Mary into His own hands, and filled her with light, and folded her to His own bosom. Her early years were devoted to His service in the temple, where an uninterrupted contemplation of the divine perfections was the food and solace of her whole being. And when the auspicious hour arrived, and the Word was made flesh in her womb, it was only a fitting reward for that incessant desire with which she had sought Him. As in all things she renounced herself, and looked alone to His power, so every action of her life was a prayer going directly to His heart. The faith and all-consuming love with which she looked upon her child were ever the most sublime acts of contemplation. And day by day she drew nearer to perfect conformity with the divine model visibly before her. As the prayer of His creatures goes up to His throne, and is heard amid the music of cherubim and seraphim, so did He on earth ever accept Mary's sweet worship. It was dearer to Him than the hosannas of heaven. When He went upon the duties of His ministry she was left to the consolation of prayer, and was able to keep up her uninterrupted communion with Him in all His wanderings and sufferings.

The great hour of man's redemption found her upon Mount Calvary, there to learn a new lesson in her wonderful power of prayer, and to be sprinkled with the blood of her Son, that she might begin her great work of intercession. Mary was the only light on earth in that dark hour, when the whole human race seemed to seek the death of its God. That death opened anew the fountains of the divine charity, and the afflicted mother, feeling the efficacy of those dying agonies, lifted up to heaven her supplication for guilty man. Her pleading words ascended, mingled with the pitying cry, "Father, forgive them, for they know not what they do." The whole life of the Blessed Virgin was solitary. When Jesus was with her nothing else could be present, and when He was taken from her she could think of nothing but Him. After the ascension the holy places of Jerusalem were her favorite resort. She sought the steps of the way of sorrows that she might retrace all the stages of the passion. Calvary and the sepulchre were quiet retreats where the remembrances of her child renewed in her soul both the sorrows and the consolations of her martyrdom. She passed in ecstacy to Him to whom she was wholly united, and the day of her assumption but lifted her body to the sacred heart on which she had rested. Her prayer is now the crown of all the intercessions of heaven, and angels and archangels wait in silence when she opens the lips which "are as a dropping honeycomb." For "honey and milk are under her tongue, and the smell of her garments as the smell of frankincencense." To her the poor sinner looks with hope, for if her lips do but plead his cause, the graces of heaven fall like dew upon his soul. It is her office, now that she is inseparable from her Son, to pray for the souls for whom He died, and for the kingdom which He has established on earth; that kingdom over which He reigns, and which His human heart ever draws nearer and nearer to His sacred person. So in truth Mary is one of the greatest consolations of our religion, not only as she guides us by her example in every way of holiness, but also as her prayers encircle the soul that seeks for God, and never fail in the hour of battle and danger. And let man offend the divine majesty as he will, her heart alway sends up its sweet sacrifice to make reparation for our countless ingratitudes.

The beautiful spirit of prayer which the

Blessed Virgin thus exhibited, may through God's mercy incite us to seek a union with her heart, and through her with the heart of Jesus. To see Him whom we love alway before our eyes, and in each action to seek His favor, is to pray without ceasing. This habit of recollection will drive away distractions from our devotions, and make the state of prayer habitual, while it will open to us new treasures in the mercy which has redeemed us. Let us call upon God at all times, and especially in the hour of temptation. And why should not His goodness allure us to follow on in the path of prayer, till the vision of faith is enlarged, and the spiritual world becomes our familiar abode? This path leads to joys no stranger can know, to perfect union with Him whose embrace is bliss inconceivable,—who desires to espouse our souls, that we may have no lover but Him. This is the path of every christian, and the mountain heights to which it guides are open to every heart that really longs and seeks after God.

CHAPTER XXXII.

THE UNION OF THE BLESSED VIRGIN WITH GOD.

"His left hand is under my head, and His right hand shall embrace me."—CANTICLES, viii. 3.

THE reflections which we have made upon the life and virtues of the holy mother of God, have at least convinced us that her praises can never worthily be celebrated by any human language. She is a creature exalted far above all the works of the Almighty, approaching so near the eternal throne, that she is lost in the glory which surrounds it. Her ways put on the mystery which belongs to the divine counsels, and her virtues assume proportions far above the reach of our conception. Her joys are like the bliss which attends the infinite perfections of God, her sorrows partake of that unapproachable woe which overwhelmed the incarnate Word, and her glories borrow the radiance of that city which the divine being perfectly illuminates. She stands alone in the history of our race, without an equal and without comparison. And the reason of her great exaltation is not only her maternal relation to her creator, but her entire union with Him through the power of His grace. To this must be ascribed her bliss on earth and her peerless crown in heaven. This union was complete and entire, and the touching verses of the Canticles feebly describe the raptures of that love which bound her to her Beloved, the power of that beauty which drew Him to her embrace. In her heart there never had been for one instant anything but devotion to Him, and her race had been run with speed far surpassing the flight of the angels. She came up from the desert of this sinful world, leaning upon her child, flowing with delights, " with her head like carmel, and the hairs of her head as the purple of the king bound in the channels." God could not sufficiently reward her great sanctity, and so He lavished upon her the profusion of His gifts. He became her child, and then took her to His arms and held her to His bosom. We poor sinners look up dazzled at the sight, even as the traveler stands in awe at the foot of the mountain which bathes its head in the distant heaven. But Mary is our dearest mother, and her heart yearns for us while we are pilgrims in this valley of tears. She beckons to us to follow her footsteps. She begs us to seek a thorough purification from our sins, and then opening wide the eternal gates, she points to the goal of all true ambition. Seek, my children, conformity with God, and never rest in your warfare till you have laid every foe prostrate, and find union with the author of your being. Seek your perfection in every trial of life, in every joy which illumines your pathway, and be never satisfied till you, like me, lay your head upon the breast of Jesus, and His right arm holds you safe forever.

It is not too much for us to seek union with God. It is the end of the Christian life, and anything less will never satisfy our souls. Any lower aim will make our journey long and bitter, and its end uncertain. We may deceive ourselves, but we can never cheat our all-seeing judge of that which is His due. To perfectly fulfill God's law is the condition of salvation, now that the stream of life flows at our feet, and the sacraments all around us are working their miracles of grace. To different hearts God manifests His will with different attractions, but all He calls to peace and union with Himself. Is it too much to hope that our meditations upon the life of Mary will stir up our energies and allure us even to the heights of virtue? God can do nothing more to move our wills or render the narrow path inviting. If Jesus and Mary do not draw us by their very loveliness, there can be no place for us in heaven. And if in reality we seek for entire union, and love which casts out all fear, then faithfully must we walk on, as the celestial spouse may lead us. We ascend by degrees. We travel on step by step, and little by little make progress in the divine life. There is no cause for discouragement when temptations crowd upon us, and darkness takes from our souls their wonted consolations. We seek God for His own sake, and not for any of His gifts. Heaven itself would be nothing without Him, and anything less than Himself would never fill p our desire. If we only correspond with His graces, we cannot be separated from Him, and sooner or later we must rest in the bosom of His love. Sin in all its effects must be utterly driven from our hearts, for He can never accept a divided affection. There must be no attachment to sin which is so offensive to Him. There must be sincere contrition for all past transgressions, and the spirit of penance which seeks to efface every vestige of former disobedience. There must be a firm and unrelenting purpose to do the divine will in all things, great or small, and the moment that it is manifested to us. We must set a high value upon the inspirations of the Holy Spirit, and fear to be careless or unfaithful, lest the blessed Comforter be grieved and speak to us no longer. We must learn to hate sin with all the intensity of our souls, and to regard it as the only evil that could befall us. With such dispositions we shall be safe, and our pilgrimage will surely lead us to the desired end. It is wonderful what grace will do in souls that are free, and well disposed. The blood of Christ washes away every defilement, and makes the sinner whiter than snow, while like a healing ointment it goes down into every wound and gives health to the exhausted energies. The divine word like a fruitful seed is planted in the heart and springs up in luxuriance and beauty. One by one all defects and imperfections pass away, and virtues take strong and deathless roots, till the man is transformed into the likeness of the Son of God. Though he know it not, and is never allowed to measure his progress, he is changing day by day, putting off the old man with all his sinful lusts, and putting on the new man with his victorious power over death and hell. The veil which hides God's counsels gradually melts away according to the words of the apostle. "When they shall be converted to the Lord, the veil shall be taken away. For where the Spirit of the Lord is, there is liberty. But we all beholding the glory of the Lord with face uncovered, are transformed into the same image from glory to glory, as by the Spirit of the Lord."* For growth is a law of life, and life coming from God bears us to Him again, who is life unchanging and eternal. We need not be anxious about the means by which the jealous lover of souls seeks to accomplish His work in us. He alone can fathom our want and put His finger upon the cause of our malady. He will keep us humble and patient by the very mode of our sanctification, and He will go before us to remove every obstacle. Light will come whenever it is good for us, and consolations will not be withheld when we can bear them. We shall find peace and rest even on earth, cleanness of conscience, and tranquillity, which is a foretaste of that

* 2 Cor., iii. 16-18.

bliss with which one day the presence of God will fill our souls. Behold then the way of life, the way of the immaculate, the path which Jesus has marked out, and which Mary has trod. It is open to all, and is our sure way to heaven.

www.ingramcontent.com/pod-product-compliance
Lightning Source LLC
Chambersburg PA
CBHW020802230426
43666CB00007B/811